NEW DIRECTIONS FOR ADULT AND CONTINUING EDUCATION

Susan Imel, *Ohio State University*
COEDITOR-IN-CHIEF

Jovita M. Ross-Gordon, *Southwest Texas State University*
COEDITOR-IN-CHIEF

Environmental Adult Education

Ecological Learning, Theory, and Practice for Socioenvironmental Change

Lilian H. Hill
Virginia Commonwealth University

Darlene E. Clover
University of Victoria

EDITORS

Number 99, Fall 2003

JOSSEY-BASS
San Francisco

ENVIRONMENTAL ADULT EDUCATION: ECOLOGICAL LEARNING, THEORY, AND PRACTICE FOR SOCIOENVIRONMENTAL CHANGE
Lilian H. Hill, Darlene E. Clover (eds.)
New Directions for Adult and Continuing Education, no. 99
Susan Imel, Jovita M. Ross-Gordon, Coeditors-in-Chief

Microfilm copies of issues and articles are available in 16mm and 35mm, as well as microfiche in 105mm, through University Microfilms Inc., 300 North Zeeb Road, Ann Arbor, Michigan 48106-1346.

ISSN 1052-2891   electronic ISSN 1536-0717

NEW DIRECTIONS FOR ADULT AND CONTINUING EDUCATION is part of The Jossey-Bass Higher and Adult Education Series and is published quarterly by Wiley Subscription Services, Inc., A Wiley company, at Jossey-Bass, 989 Market Street, San Francisco, California 94103-1741. Periodicals postage paid at San Francisco, California, and at additional mailing offices. Postmaster: Send address changes to New Directions for Adult and Continuing Education, Jossey-Bass, 989 Market Street, San Francisco, California, 94103-1741.

SUBSCRIPTIONS cost $70.00 for individuals and $149.00 for institutions, agencies, and libraries.

EDITORIAL CORRESPONDENCE should be sent to the Coeditors-in-Chief, Susan Imel, ERIC/ACVE, 1900 Kenny Road, Columbus, Ohio 43210-1090. e-mail: imel.l@osu.edu, or Jovita M. Ross-Gordon, Southwest Texas State University, EAPS Dept., 601 University Drive, San Marcos, TX 78666.

Cover photograph by Wernher Krutein/PHOTOVAULT © 1990.

www.josseybass.com

CONTENTS

EDITORS' NOTES   1
Lilian H. Hill, Darlene E. Clover

1. Environmental Adult Education: Critique and Creativity in   5
a Globalizing World
Darlene E. Clover
Emerging principles and practices of environmental adult education
provide a contemporary lens through which adult educators can examine globalization and make stronger links to grassroots and global
activism.

2. Adult Education and Humanity's Relationship with Nature   17
Reflected in Language, Metaphor, and Spirituality: A Call to
Action
Lilian H. Hill, Julie D. Johnston
By reexamining our use of language and creating new metaphors, envi-
ronmental adult educators can rebuild spiritual relationships with the
rest of nature.

3. Environmental Justice: Environmental Adult Education at   27
the Confluence of Oppressions
Robert J. Hill
To be most effective, environmental adult education must include a
social justice framework that addresses environmental racism and helps
to build more equitable and democratic societies.

4. Environmental Adult Education and Community   39
Sustainability
Jennifer Sumner
The author presents ideas for a new framework of sustainability for
adult education that can help communities survive and thrive in the age
of globalization.

5. Environmental Popular Education and Indigenous Social   47
Movements in India
Dip Kapoor
Practical and theoretical considerations regarding environmental pop-
ular education with and for indigenous peoples struggling against
destructive development practices in India are explored.

6. Environmental Adult Education: Women Living the   59
Tensions
Lee Karlovic, Kathryn Patrick
The authors describe women's ecological learning in a workshop that
moved them beyond a focus on individual change toward the connections between environmental problems, media and marketing, and
activism.

7. Words for the World: Creating Critical Environmental   69
Literacy for Adults
Ralf St. Clair
Moving away from a focus on scientific knowledge, environmental
adult literacy taps into the ecological wisdom of learners and stimulates
more critical engagement.

8. Learning Environments and Environmental Education   79
Paul Bélanger
An exploration of the concepts of an ecology of learning and learning
environments can challenge ongoing antienvironmental practices in
today's educational systems.

9. Learning Patterns of Landscape and Life   89
Darlene E. Clover, Lilian H. Hill
Drawing together the main themes of the chapters, the volume's editors
highlight the importance of the ecological dimension in adult education in today's world and provide suggestions for further reading.

INDEX   97

Editors' Notes

Why is it important to discuss environmental issues in the context of adult and continuing education? Many of the world's adults are very much aware of environmental problems and are afraid, in fact terrified, that the world is in immediate danger. Their understandings come from a variety of sources such as personal observations and daily lived experiences, their peers, news reports and other media, and community-action campaigns. However, environmental problems loom large and can be difficult to understand due to both their scientific nature, and more importantly, the complexity of ideological standpoints at their origin. The latter barrier makes it difficult for people to envision how they can possibly make a difference, thereby engendering feelings of hopelessness, fear, confusion, and apathy.

More educational opportunities are required in order for adults to come together and collectively share experiences and learn from each other, challenge assumptions and discursive norms, and create new knowledge for socioenvironmental change. Environmental adult education is one framework within which adult educators can facilitate collective learning opportunities for adults around ecological concerns in order to formulate concrete responses.

Extensive education programming and literature already exists for children, yet environmental concerns have been largely neglected in adult education discourse and practice. Discussions on environmental adult and popular education have been frequent in nations and regions of the world outside of North America. This volume represents a collaborative effort between scholars residing in Canada and the United States, many of whom have international origins, experiences, and perspectives, to illumine this vital subject for adult educators. Environmental adult education is inextricably linked with concerns already receiving much needed attention, including (1) oppression based on race, gender, sexual orientation, socioeconomic class, ethnicity, religion, and national origin, (2) citizen participation, democracy, and civil society, and (3) social action. Environmental and social injustices are intertwined within a complex and intimate, interdependent relationship, and neither form of injustice can be adequately addressed or acted upon in the absence of the other.

The first three chapters of this sourcebook lay the foundations for environmental adult education. In Chapter One, Darlene E. Clover explains the scope of environmental adult education and situates the need for it firmly in a discussion of pernicious globalizing processes that negatively affect the environment and the quality of people's lives worldwide. Further, she argues that environmental deterioration is an issue that affects everyone—it is a cultural issue, a political issue, a social issue, a feminist issue, a global issue.

Environmental adult educators need to become activists, strengthen democracy, and forge strong links with community groups.

How people use language and metaphor to express their beliefs about their relationship with the natural world is the topic tackled by Lilian H. Hill and Julie D. Johnston in Chapter Two. Relationships embedded in a limited modern worldview separate humanity from the natural world, and this fallacy renders people nearly incapable of perceiving the causal factors of environmental decline. Adult educators can make it possible for students and participant collaborators to widen their perceptions to reconnect within the natural world of which we are an integral part. A spirituality of meaning and purpose can prompt humanity to heal the self-created alienation between people and the natural world. It is a call to action required for survival of the earth and all its beings.

Environmental justice, the complex and vital issue raised by Robert J. Hill in Chapter Three, acknowledges colluding factors of racism, classism, sexism, and hegemony that underlie environmental deterioration and worsening health of marginalized and oppressed populations locally and globally. Popular education and social movement learning are vital for people to name and combat inequity, and environmental adult education serves a crucial role by building environmental democracy. Environmental justice learning that leads to social transformation and more equitable conditions is critical to revitalizing a healthy ecology.

In Chapter Four, Jennifer Sumner links environmental adult education and community sustainability. The health of communities remains a critical issue in a globalizing world. Connection to place and life in community influence our relationship within the environment and help us relearn what people need for healthy living, working, and relating to one another and the earth. Environmental learning linked to life values, critical reflection, and dialogue engenders new ways of seeing and being in the world. Environmental adult education, grounded in the local and reaching out to other localities, can engender a global pedagogy of community sustainability.

Adult educator activists using environmental popular education to work with indigenous peoples is the topic raised by Dip Kapoor in Chapter Five. Indigenous peoples living on every continent cannot be easily subsumed into a single discussion. In his discussion of indigenous social movements in India, Kapoor considers practical and theoretical implications related to the use of popular education within social movements that are dedicated to opposing environmental displacement and oppression.

Women living the tensions between their environmental convictions and daily, pragmatic ethical choices is the subject of Chapter Six by Lee Karlovic and Kathryn Patrick. In a variety of ways, women are most affected by socioenvironmental degradation. Karlovic and Patrick choose one example of a group of seven women, with more than seventy-five years' collective experience in adult and popular education, who came together to explore intricate and complex connections between women, the environment, and adult education.

In Chapter Seven, Ralf St. Clair identifies and reflects on the challenges of environmental literacy. Before universal environmental literacy can be realized, the challenges of both literacy education and environmental literacy must be addressed. The need to convey key scientific concepts more accessibly, redress the dominance of government and "objective" science, acknowledge and value the experience of diverse peoples, and finally link experience to action provide substantial challenges to environmental adult education. Reconnecting the word and the world will not be simple or easy. St. Clair concludes that critically applying the metaphor of literacy to environmental challenges we face allows us to participate in changing social practices in the way we think about and act in the environment.

In Chapter Eight, Paul Bélanger proposes a new ecology of learning that confronts ongoing beliefs and practices in environmental education. Environmental education programming for adults has historically been paid too little attention, is often underfunded, and is frequently conceived as a public, one-way communication campaign. Creation of collective, social dialogue and significant learning opportunities linking local conditions to global issues is essential. An ecological understanding of learning involves adults connecting environmental learning to personal experiences in the environment, a focus on local problems and ecological risks, a lifelong learning orientation, and societal interaction and dialogue.

The editors close with a final chapter that summarizes inescapable themes addressed in this sourcebook: the pernicious effects of globalization, the interdependent entanglements of oppression of the earth and all its beings, and the need for opportunities and spaces within which to explore and challenge environmental deterioration. Environmental adult education taking place in social movements, communities, organizations, and classrooms begins with respect for ecological knowledge and attention to local contexts and conditions. Through a diversity of practices, it responds both emotionally and cognitively to ecological issues within the context of social and global concerns. To be effective, environmental adult education cannot be an isolated intellectual exercise. Instead, shared knowledge, dialogue, and social action are central to transformative ecological learning that connects us within the natural world and enables us to act for the survival and revitalization of all life.

Lilian H. Hill
Darlene E. Clover
Editors

LILIAN H. HILL is education specialist and assistant professor at Virginia Commonwealth University in Richmond, Virginia.

DARLENE E. CLOVER is assistant professor of adult education in the Faculty of Education, University of Victoria, British Columbia.

1

This chapter explores the links between war, social unrest, natural resources, and globalization and raises contemporary issues of environmental racism and sexism. Environmental adult education provides a space to examine the negative environmental impacts experienced by people worldwide and to refocus on democracy, accountability, creativity, and action.

Environmental Adult Education: Critique and Creativity in a Globalizing World

Darlene E. Clover

Contemporary capitalist globalization has a powerful impact on every aspect of human life. Economics, public policy, education, work, agriculture, and culture are all affected by the incessant drive to accumulate wealth. Globalization has also enabled Western capitalist nations to dominate and destroy natural environments like never before. The much promoted paperless and wireless knowledge economy has done nothing to diminish the current globalizing project's need for natural resources. This need has made a lucky few very rich, endangered the lives and livelihoods of countless others, and lies at the root of wars and social breakdown worldwide.

Since globalization has an impact on every part of people's lives, adult educators need to analyze, critique, and challenge it from a variety of standpoints. In this chapter I explore globalization through the lens of environmental adult education. I begin by examining four core ecological implications of globalization: (1) war and social instability, (2) production and consumption, (3) corporatization and marketing, and (4) environmental racism and sexism. This is followed by a brief overview of some of the concepts that frame environmental adult education and an array of global practices that respect ecological knowledge(s), encourage creativity, and stimulate debate and dialogue around contemporary environmental problems. To be most effective, environmental adult education must be linked to local, national, or global activism and be based in a discourse of democracy, accountability, equity, and hope.

NEW DIRECTIONS FOR ADULT AND CONTINUING EDUCATION, no. 99, Fall 2003 © Wiley Periodicals, Inc.

Environmental Issues in the Fabric of Capitalist Globalization

The scientific and industrial revolutions enabled Western capitalist nations to dominate cultures, politics, and environments. However, contemporary globalization, through lightning speed and intense interconnectivity, has affected far greater changes to society and ecology (Stromquist and Monkman, 2000). While definitions of globalization vary significantly, there seem to be four salient features. First, globalization is "the latest form of capitalist reorganization" (Mayo, 1999, p. 1) that shapes society through an "alliance of modern science, technology and markets" (Byrne and Glover, 2002, p. 7). Second, it erodes the "barriers of time and space that constrain human activity" (p. 7) and "trivializes what is small, particular, indigenous and local" (Harris, 1996, p. 8). Third, it has an impact on all aspects of life: the economy, work force, communications, education, culture, health, language and literacy, governance, and the environment (Stromquist and Monkman, 2000). Fourth, as globalization increasingly penetrates the life-world, people become more aware of its impact on the "'every-day' of life" (Byrne and Glover, 2002, p. 8). While the first three features have quite negative connotations, the final one stirs hope and promise.

When First Nations educator Peter Cole (1998) questions in his poetic essay "who is benefiting from cash crop cultures; why is there no talk of shell oil and starbucks; why should globalisation mean poor people in Kenya go without rice; because of a war in Iraq" (p. 103), he makes a poignant link between the environment and globalization. The ideological underpinnings of globalization of increased competition, production, marketing, privatization, and deregulation—all in the single-minded pursuit of wealth—have created massive ecological imbalances of unprecedented proportion. People and ecosystems that find themselves on the *periphery* of global capital are at best "treated as appendages to the growth requirements" (Bellamy Foster, 1994, p. 85), or what is worse, as dispensable commodities.

Death, War, and Natural Resources

Karl Marx argued in 1844 that the world depends on the "products of nature, whether they appear in the form of food, heating, clothes, a dwelling." The environment is the "direct means of life . . . and instrument of life-activity" (cited in Tucker, 1972, p. 75). Little has changed. Capitalist globalization remains dependent upon the world's natural resources to sustain and propel itself forward and in doing so, causes a devastating scarcity for those it displaces. The new knowledge economy of paperless and wireless technologies and communications has in no way diminished this fact, it has merely facilitated resource allocation and extraction.

Globalization has created fundamental problems of livelihood, equity, sustainability, and justice (Appadurai, 2001). Struggles to obtain and maintain control of natural resources are escalating worldwide. The majority of wars are fought not over ideology, but territory, land that is rich in natural resources. One example is the multi-year civil war in Sierra Leone over control of the country's diamond mines. While thousands of innocent people are killed or forced to flee their homeland, foreign-owned corporations make tidy profits. A second example is the contestations around Iraq. Regardless of the hyperbole of "ridding the world of tyranny," making things "safe," and "caring" for the "oppressed," the instability is about the fundamental need for an indispensable natural resource—oil. This fact is recognized by progressive leaders such as Nelson Mandela and the thousands of antiwar protesters who chant slogans of "Hell no, we won't die for Texaco" and "No blood for oil."

Globalization in general, and the excessive exploration of natural resources in particular, has forced many people around the world to live in degradation and poverty. As rural peasants and farmers are moved and pushed off fertile lands onto marginal ones, social infrastructures break down. Moreover, people who have attempted to protect their land or resources against the ravishes of globalization often pay a high price. One example comes from the Greenbelt Movement in Africa. Founder Wangari Maathai has been tireless in her critiques of development practices that rob citizens of parkland and natural resources. For this work, she has been the target of government repression, often undergoing physical beating and imprisonment (Clover, 1995). Two other and more extreme examples come from Niger and Brazil. In Nigeria, Ken Saro-Wiwa and his colleagues were executed "as a result of their campaign against the environmental destruction of their homeland by Shell" (Horseman, quoted in Clover, 2002, p. 321). In Brazil, nineteen landless peasants from the Landless Rural Workers Movement were massacred. In spite of this, "organizing, consciousness-raising and mobilization for the rights of the poorest of the poor" continues (Lowy, 2001, p. 32).

Production, Consumption, and Marketing

One of the major debates within the environmental movement is the very cornerstone of capitalist globalization: production and consumption. While environmentalists most often focus on the downstream activity of consumption, the upstream activity is very much in need of closer examination.

Production is the creation of saleable goods, most of which come directly from natural resources. Even synthetic products draw on something from the environment, since little is conjured from thin air. The process of production reflects the ways in which humans interact with each other and the rest of nature. In precapitalist economies—a few of which still exist today—people engaged in production activities as direct, reciprocal, personal relations of exchange. While not perfect, these economies were based on the philosophy that "those who need, receive, and those who can, give. . . . There were no poor and needy in comparison with other members and likewise, no wealthy and privileged" (Rowe, 2002, p. 56). The great change today is that the majority of interactions, particularly in the mainstream market, are based upon producing items for exchange and profit.

Von Moltke (1997) argues that "it is not happenstance that the most important environmental threats today (global warming, biodiversity loss, wholesale ecosystem modification, and toxic pollution) can be traced directly to production of commodities and commodity manufactures" (p. 38). Capitalist production is about changing raw materials or natural resources into saleable commodities. Living is reduced to a competition, and all relations among humans and between humans and the rest of nature are seen as economic relationships. Both human value and the value of the rest of nature are subordinate to the values of a world market that treats everything as a commodity.

The contemporary metamorphosis of consumption from an act of pillage and destruction, as it was once labeled, to an act of virtue and prestige "is one of the most important yet least examined phenomena of the twentieth century" (Rifkin, 1996, p. 19). Beginning particularly in the 1950s, the Western world began to see an "unprecedented growth of a consumer society; a term which signifies not just affluence and the expansion of production and markets, but also the increasing penetration of the meaning and images associated with consumption into the culture of everyday life" (Clover, 2002, p. 80).

The more people consumed, the higher their standard of living, and by association, their quality of life. In fact "forced consumerism was extolled: things had to be consumed, burned, used, replaced and discarded at a constantly accelerating pace" (Lahaye, 1995, p. 60).

Consumerism taunts society with the idea of scarcity, appeals to competitiveness, and mimics the tensions of seasonal rarity (Griffiths, 1997). It represents a crisis of values and meaning. Consumerism is gendered practice and a discourse through which power is both exercised and contested.

For some, consumerism is seen as a "behavioral" problem calling for education to be targeted toward the individual. However, for others, consumerism is viewed as a deeply ingrained ideological, political, and structural problem given strength through advertising. The media-marketing machine today is the single most pervasive form of informal learning, focusing on creating need and orchestrating ignorance. As advertising executive Jacques Duval (1995) argues, advertising "boils down to boosting sales of a product in a particular market, and thus to encouraging consumption . . . to claim otherwise would be a lie" (p. 59). Focusing solely on the individual—although many agree that consumers have a certain degree of power—depoliticizes and privatizes a very political and public issue.

Corporatization

Another aspect of globalization is corporatization. The speed of foreign takeover of small business enterprises by large corporations is staggering.

Hectares of fertile farmland and small, local shops give way to predominantly American-owned megastores and fast-food outlets. The health risks of increased obesity associated with contemporary fast-food diets are becoming apparent. The packaging and waste from the literally millions of items sold creates more and more rubbish sites. Moreover, the forming of unions in these locations is deeply discouraged, if not totally forbidden.

Educator/activist Tony Clarke (1997) argues that "it is probably fair to say that there was a higher degree of political literacy . . . about corporations and the power they wield 25 years ago than there is today. Back then, the press and air waves were filled with lively debates about foreign ownership. . . . In more recent years, however, there has been surprisingly little analysis of the political influence of modern corporations over governments today and about what to do about it" (p. 5).

Corporations are lobbying gurus, and newspapers and other mainstream media that are monopoly-owned and dependent on advertising help them to "maintain a certain amount of public control" and cover up "pollution and human rights abuses" (Clover, 2001, p. 82). Transnational corporations also have the ability to control costs, prices, labor, and materials (Harris, 1996).

The global economy survives on its ability to make and sell more and more goods that are derived from natural resources, either directly or indirectly. To increase profit, corporate advertising has become more and more aggressive and sophisticated.

Environmental Sexism and Racism

Globalization has "eroded not only the nation state's ability to control their own monetary and fiscal policies, but also their economic and political sovereignty" (Harris, 1996, p. 7). One manifestation of this is a major decrease in expenditures on health care, education, social welfare and antipoverty programs, and environmental protection.

For many women, degradation of the environment is a matter of life and death for themselves, their children, and their communities. The loss of forests in India due to excessive logging means women walk miles each day to gather fuel supplies and water. Dry riverbeds or bacteria-infested water systems mean illness and often death for children and the elderly, both of whom are cared for primarily by women (see Cuomo, 1998; Mies and Shiva, 1993).

Women are also caught up in the consumption and marketing game. In most societies, women make the primary purchases for the home—which include everything from food to cleaning supplies, sheets to lunch boxes. The advertising industry knows this. It aggressively targets them to "buy specific products such as those that keep their families 'free from germs,'" and as primary purchasers and targets of advertising women are constantly blamed for "poor" consumer choices "which harm not only their families, but [also] the entire planet!" (Clover, Follen, and Hall, 2000,

p. 58). Feminist educators have also discovered that even so-called "green consumerism" does nothing to challenge economic growth and brings "women's lives under scrutiny in a new private ecological morality" (Sandilands, 1993, p. 46).

The politics and practice of environmental racism are also deeply embedded in capitalism and globalization. As adult educator Mikkes David Lengwati (1995) articulates so well, "when minerals like gold, diamonds, platinum and coal are extracted but the surrounding communities are among the poorest in the country; when black townships experience the leakage of water pipes and sewers without any hope of the local government attending to repairs; when black township streets lack sheltering trees for shade and ornamental flowers for beautification; and when blacks-only areas are targeted as industrial sites . . . racism is clear" (p. 103). Aboriginal peoples around the world do not have "control over their Traditional Territories" and often "face devastating environmental degradation" that has a major impact on "their ways of life, knowledge systems, traditional governance systems, food, and cultures" (Simpson, 2002, pp. 13–14).

Environmental Adult Education

Like globalization and adult education, there is no single definition of environmental adult education. Rather, as I discovered through an international comparative study, there seem to be a number of commonly shared conceptual frameworks and strategies (Clover, 1999).

Environmental adult education makes concrete links between the environment and social, economic, political, and cultural aspects of people's lives. For example, when fisheries collapse due to overfishing in places where the folklore is based upon a life of the sea, people's economic worlds and cultural identities are destabilized.

Environmental adult education is an engaged and participatory process of political and social learning and not solely a matter of individual behavior change and information transmission. While individuals can and should make changes in their lifestyles, the most toxic environmental problems result from the practice of capitalist globalization. While awareness-raising frameworks of public education focus on keeping people informed on matters of pollution, science, and technology, environmental adult education uses engaged, participatory methods based on the understanding that learning is a far more complex, extensive, and important process than information transmission. Environmental adult education begins from a platform of recognizing people's ecological knowledge(s) and bringing these together through dialogue and debate to create new ecological understandings of our world. This also includes respecting and weaving into the learning process spiritualities and ways of knowing and being that are linked to the land.

Environmental adult education is about root causes and is therefore deeply critical of market- and consumer-driven capitalism/globalization, but not of citizens. It is also a process that is community-oriented and contextually shaped. This does not mean that communities are simply accepted as is, but rather working toward the democratization of power by challenging underlying racial, class, and gender biases and other inequities.

Humans make their world by learning and participating in its being. Their ideas and theories are grounded in the life-world, emerging from experience and ritual. Environmental adult education uses a variety of critical and creative practices, strategies, and tools in the praxis of learning.

Practices of Environmental Adult Education

While globalization generates acute global problems, there is also a "positive force that encourages an emancipatory politics of globalization"—the imagination (Appadurai, 2001, p. 6). The imagination allows people to resist state and corporate violence, seek social and environmental redress, critique and challenge and design new forms of civic engagement, collaboration and learning (Appadurai, 2001), and gives "credence to alternative realities" (Greene, 1995, p. 3). Through their practice in social movements, universities, colleges, communities, and nongovernmental organizations, environmental adult educators demonstrate and unlock the powers of critical engagement and the imagination.

Social Movement Learning. A central component to antiglobalization actions around the world are "teach-ins." Teach-ins bring together students, the elderly, artists, educators, activists, and union members to discuss strategies and explore troubling issues such as genetically modified foods, trade and the environment, militarism and corporatization, poverty, and democracy. The Polaris Institute in Ottawa, Canada, supplies learning materials to teach-ins in order to "develop leadership capacities for economic justice" (Clarke and Dopp, 2001, p. 4).

Universities and Colleges. Footprints International at the University of Calgary created a program based on popular theater. This critical and entertaining educational tool helped people to examine issues of consumerism, sustainability, and the exploitation of natural resources (Keough, Carmona, and Grandinetti, 1995). An adult education course at Loyalist College in Belleville, Ontario, uses trips to megastores and large grocery chains to discuss connections between waste, packaging, and advertising; gender socialization through toys; and the genetic modification of our foods (Clover, 2001). At the University of Waikato in New Zealand, adult education students wove together theoretical debates on environmental issues, aboriginal rights, and adult education with hands-on research and experiential community learning (Stalker, 1995).

Communities and Nongovernmental Organizations. On Vancouver Island, Canada, a group of women artists organized a creative learning process using "needle and thread" to protest a Canada-America partnership to build a gas-fired power plant. Bringing together over sixty people, a series of quilts were collectively created to provoke dialogue around the environment, U.S. corporate takeover in particular, and governmental responsibility (Miller, 2002). In Uganda, the Multi-Purpose Training and Employment Association runs an ecological literacy program for women that focuses on problematic gender relations, and teaches reading and writing by rooting it in the landscape and using local materials. This learning process weaves a tapestry of women's knowledge and food, inequity, and change and uses both song and theater (Young People of the World, 1999). The Toronto Chinese Health Education Committee challenges environmental racism by ascribing to a "philosophy that ecological healing comes through the revitalization of the vision, strength and moral values" of all communities (Tan, 2003).

Based on a belief that adult learning is about working with people to challenge and create, environmental adult educators use the arts and dialogue, debate and experience, resistance and the land to tackle complex, contemporary issues.

Activism and the Environmental Adult Educator

Citizens young and old are becoming increasingly more politically active and speaking out, weaving the pedagogical with the political. First Nations educators in Canada include the idea of "resistance" in their work, thereby injecting "the learning process with power and hope, with the recognition that peoples have worked hard to protect our traditional lands" (Simpson, 2002, p. 19). Actors in the antiglobalization movement form global alliances to challenge corporate takeover and stimulate dialogue around basic notions of governance and democracy. In Escravos, Nigeria, in 2002, a group of women "took over a giant oil terminal and trapped hundreds of workers inside. . . . They did not budge in their demands for jobs for their sons and electricity for their homes. Tempers flared during the talks held in a sweltering village of rusty tin shacks only 100 yards from the looming concrete terminal, where 700 employees . . . [were] trapped for six days" (D. Doran, Associated Press, e-mail to the author, July 2002).

While not all their demands were met, corporate officials did agree to hire at least five people and to build a town hall, schools, and electrical and water systems. On February 1, 2003, a number of seniors—all in their eighties and nineties—from the Redwood Retirement Center in California came out to protest George Bush leading the country into war. "Using canes, walkers, and wheelchairs," they created a counternarrative of resistance that questioned the dominant agenda of violence (Whitaker, 2003, p. 1).

Feminist environmental adult educator Moema Viezzer (1992) once suggested that in order to best facilitate the emergence of ecological perspectives and knowledges, adult educators should create learning cultures and build stronger networks and partnerships with social movements. Since the actions of social movements have been crucial in challenging capitalism's negative impact on equity, justice, and the environment, environmental adult educators, particularly within institutions, need to become activists.

Linking education and activism creates a symbiotic educational opportunity for both practitioners and learners. The benefits flow in both directions and are mutually dependent for their existence. Forging stronger links between environmental adult educators and community groups and movements can help create more workable strategies and achieve mutual goals. In particular, the environmental movement has not understood well either how people learn or the full importance of education to their work (Whelan, 2000). And while environmental adult educators should not "supplant existing educational efforts of environmental groups" they can help broaden and democratize them (Jansen, 1995, p. 95). In reaching out to environmental groups, adult educators can introduce inclusive, participatory educational practices that emerge from the principles of environmental adult education.

Democracy and State Responsibility

Antiglobalization actions around the world demonstrate that citizens have developed a capacity to challenge corporate power and relate to global institutions such as the United Nations. However, activism and protests are no substitute for democratic governance. And the political arena remains the space in which most of the power lies.

Democracy is in the process of being reduced to casting a ballot once every four or five years, or participating in a series of endless political referendums or market polls. Even in societies with longstanding democratic traditions, such as Canada, democracy is under threat and there are high levels of citizen disillusionment. Contemporary forces of globalization have found ways to blind the public through prescriptive marketing and monopoly-owned media, and, as mentioned before, limit the effectiveness and power of national governments. For example, nations no longer have the power to regulate exchange or interest rates and are therefore less able to insist on social accountability from corporations (Harris, 1996). Having said this, it is also important to recognize the culpability of governments. Many Western nations push free trade, nurture business through tax reduction, encourage foreign takeover, and allow corporations to sidestep labor laws (Clarke, 1997). Therefore, it is extremely important that we inject a message of state accountability and responsibility to its citizens into our learning processes. Corporations are simply not in the business of protecting or enhancing public health (Harris, 1996). It is the role of the state, the elected officials, to ensure a "quality provision of services, guided by the principles of equity and entitlement" (Mayo, 1999, p. 3). Let's make sure they do so.

Conclusion

Globalization has had an unprecedented negative impact on the planet. This means that neither politics, economics, public policy, education, nor work, food, health care, nor immigration have been unaffected by genetic modification, deforestation, soil erosion, water and air pollution, toxic waste, climate change, fisheries collapse, oil spills, militarization, deregulation, trade, marketing, and/or urban decay.

Race, poverty, and gender are important lenses through which we shape adult education theory and practice. Environmental adult education adds another critical lens, an ecological lens through which we can address environmental problems and give voice to the needs of those who are most affected. Environmental deterioration is a cultural issue, a political issue, a feminist issue, an economic issue, a race issue, a workplace issue, a youth issue, a global issue. By keeping democracy at the forefront, making stronger links to social movements, and working at local, national, and global levels, and through persistence and imagination, dialogue, and debate, we can reassert a vision of the world we want.

References

Appadurai, A. (ed.). *Globalization*. Durham, N.C.: Duke University Press, 2001.

Bellamy Foster, J. *The Vulnerable Planet: A Short Economic History of the Environment*. New York: Monthly Review Press, 1994.

Byrne, J., and Glover, L. "A Common Future or Towards a Future Commons: Globalization and Sustainable Development Since UNCED." *International Review for Environmental Strategies*, 2002, *3*(1), 5–25.

Clarke, T. *Silent Coup: Confronting the Big Business Takeover in Canada, Ottawa and Toronto*. Ottawa: Canadian Centre for Policy Alternatives and James Lorimer, 1997.

Clarke, T., and Dopp, S. *Beyond McWorld: A Workbook for Young Activists*. Ottawa: Canadian Centre for Policy Alternatives, 2001.

Clover, D. E. "Gender, Transformative Learning, and Environmental Action." *Gender and Education*, 1995, *7*(3), 243–258.

Clover, D. E. "Towards a Theoretical Framework of Environmental Adult Education: An International Comparative Study." Unpublished doctoral thesis, Department of Adult Education, Ontario Institute for Studies of Education/University of Toronto, 1999.

Clover, D. E. "Youth Action and Learning for Sustainable Consumption in Canada." In *Youth, Consumption Patterns and Lifestyles* (pp. 73–103). Paris: UNESCO/UNEP, 2001. [www.unesco.org/education/youth_consumption].

Clover, D. E. "Traversing the Gap: Conscientazacion, Educative-Activism and Environmental Adult Education." *Environmental Education Research*, 2002, *8*(3), 315–323.

Clover, D. E., Follen, S., and Hall, B. *The Nature of Transformation: Environmental Adult Education*. (2nd ed.) Toronto: University of Toronto Press, 2000.

Cole, P. "An Academic Take on Indigenous Traditions and Ecology." *Canadian Journal of Environmental Education*, 1998, *3*, 100–115.

Cuomo, C. J. *Feminism and Ecological Communities: An Ethic of Flourishing*. London: Routledge, 1998.

Duval, J. "An Interview with Jacques Duval, Advertising Executive." *EcoDecision*, 1995, *16*, 57–59.

Greene, M. *Releasing the Imagination: Essays on Education, the Arts, and Social Change*. San Francisco: Jossey-Bass, 1995.

Griffiths, J. "Art as a Weapon of Protest." *Resurgence*, 1997, *180*, 35–37.

Harris, E. "Revisioning Citizenship for the Global Village: Implications for Adult Education." *Convergence*, 1996, *29*(4), 5–13.

Jansen, L. "Citizen Activism in the Foundations of Adult Environmental Education in the United States." *Convergence*, 1995, *28*(4), 89–98.

Keough, N., Carmona, E., and Grandinetti, L. "Tales from the Sari-Sari: In Search of Bigfoot." *Convergence,* 1995, *28*(4), 5–11.

Lahaye, M. "The Consumer and 'Green' Products." *EcoDecision,* 1995, *16,* 60–62.

Lengwati, M. D. "The Politics of Environmental Destruction and the Use of Nature as Teacher and Site of Learning." *Convergence,* 1995, *28*(4), 99–105.

Lowy, M. "The Socio-Religious Origins of Brazil's Landless Rural Workers Movement." *Monthly Review,* June 2001, *53*(2), 32–40.

Mayo, P. *Gramsci, Freire, and Adult Education: Possibilities for Transformative Action.* London: Zed Books, 1999.

Mies, M., and Shiva, V. (eds.). *Ecofeminism.* Atlantic Highlands, N.J.: Zed Books, 1993.

Miller, K. "Positive Energy Protest Quilts: A Visual Protest." Unpublished manuscript, 2002.

Rifkin, J. *The End of Work.* New York: Putman, 1996.

Rowe, S. *Home Place.* (rev. ed.) Edmonton, Canada: New West Publishers, 2002.

Sandilands, C. "On 'Green' Consumerism: Environmental Privatization and 'Family Values.'" *Canadian Women's Studies,* 1993, *13*(3), 45–47.

Simpson, L. "Indigenous Environmental Education for Cultural Survival." *Canadian Journal of Environmental Education,* 2002, *7*(1), 13–25.

Stalker, J. "Making a Change: Environmental Activism in the Academy." *Convergence,* 1995, *28*(4), 23–30.

Stromquist, N., and Monkman, K. (eds.). *Globalization and Education: Integration and Contestation Across Cultures.* Lanham, Md.: Rowman & Littlefield, 2000.

Tan, S. "Anti-Racist Environmental Adult Education in a Trans-Global Community: Case Studies from Toronto." In D. E. Clover (ed.), *Global Perspectives in Environmental Adult Education: Justice, Sustainability, and Transformation.* New York: Peter Lang, 2003.

Tucker, R. C. *The Marx-Engels Reader.* (2nd ed.) London: Norton, 1972.

Viezzer, M. "Learning for Environmental Action." *Convergence,* 1992, *25*(2), 3–8.

Von Moltke, K. "The Global Trade in Commodities: Madonna Versus Tuna." *Ecodecision,* Spring 1997, pp. 37–38.

Whelan, J. "Learning to Save the World: Observations of the Training for Effective Advocacy in the Australian Environment Movement." *Convergence,* 2000, *33*(3), 62–73.

Whitaker, T. "Mill Valley Seniors Stage Protest for Peace." *Marin Independent Journal,* Feb. 1, 2003, p. 1.

Young People of the World. *Pachamama: Our Earth—Our Future.* London: Trafalgar Square, 1999.

DARLENE E. CLOVER is assistant professor of adult education in the Faculty of Education, University of Victoria, British Columbia.

2

*Language, metaphor, and spirituality express people's
beliefs about their relationships with the natural world.
For the earth and its beings to survive, extensive changes
in our relationships and cultural assumptions in the natural world are called for, and these will necessarily
change the literature and practice of adult education.*

Adult Education and Humanity's Relationship with Nature Reflected in Language, Metaphor, and Spirituality: A Call to Action

Lilian H. Hill, Julie D. Johnston

At a recent social marketing workshop for environmental auditors, Julie (Johnston) asked participants what they were hoping to learn by the end of the day and made a list of their ideas and questions. When she suggested that the group plant these as seeds in a garden and check back later to see if they had sprouted, one of the participants whispered, "That's a nifty analogy." This was a deliberate attempt on her part to incorporate nature-oriented metaphors into the day's learning. But later, as she discussed the influence of the language choices we make, she found herself using expressions like, "If you want to be on the front line" or "In order to be in the vanguard," and suddenly everyone noticed she was using metaphors with military connotations. The dictionary offers secondary, nonmilitary meanings for both terms, but the mental images they invoke are certainly not organic. While personally mortified, she was happy to observe the workshop participants realize how insidious this type of metaphor can be.

Many adult educators are working for social change by challenging oppressive systems based on race, class, gender, and national origin. Integrating environmental issues in our critical practice extends our ability to address concerns that adult students bring to the learning environment, as Julie's story illustrates. Adult educators can foster consciousness of the value of interdependence, interconnectedness, cooperation, and valuing of diversity as central to our ability to survive and flourish in the world. O'Sullivan (1999) tells us the "fundamental educational task of our times is to make

New Directions for Adult and Continuing Education, no. 99, Fall 2003 © Wiley Periodicals, Inc.

the choice for sustainable planetary habitat of interdependent life forms over and against the dysfunctional calling of the global competitive marketplace" (p. 2). This calls for extensive changes in our conceptions of our relationships within nature, in language, use of metaphor, spiritual beliefs, and actions. These transformations will necessarily bring about change in the practice and literature of adult education.

This chapter begins with an examination of changing conceptions of humanity's place within the world. The power of language and metaphor to structure behavior and reveal people's beliefs about the natural world are explored next, followed by a discussion of the use of metaphor in adult education practice. The chapter concludes with a discussion of spirituality within adult education practice and connects it to environmental practice.

Humanity's Relationship with the Natural World

Humanity's relationship with nature is under scrutiny, and environmentalists suggest that instead of imagining that we live outside of nature and can control it, human beings must learn to see themselves as natural beings acting within nature. "This new form of learning about our place in the world poses a fundamental challenge to the Western humanist tradition which places 'Man' above nature and assigns 'him' the task of having dominion over all things" (Welton, 1993, p. 157).

The concept of "nature merely serves as a mirror onto which societies project the ideal reflections they wish to see" (Cronon, 1996, p. 36). For some, the natural world serves as a spiritual deity. For others, nature exists apart from human beings, implying that natural resources are to be exploited. Di Chiro (1996) questions what it means to talk about nature as benevolent mother, as wild spaces unspoiled by human hands, or as the place where family and community convene and share life experiences. As recognition of environmental decline becomes more widespread, environmentalists search for or "construct interpretations that integrate political, economic, and social perspectives with the psychological and spiritual process of widening the sense of self in respect to nature" (Thomashow, 1995, p. 53). "We *could* choose to think about nature differently, and it is surely worth pondering what would happen if we did" (Cronon, 1996, p. 34; emphasis in original).

Just one of several ways of thinking differently about nature, *deep ecology* recognizes the "fundamental interdependence of all phenomena and the fact that we, as individuals and societies, are embedded in and ultimately dependent on the cyclical processes of nature" (Capra, 1996, p. 6). Deep ecology reevaluates modernist perspectives on the human role in the natural world and stresses the value of all life on earth. *Ecological feminism* shares much with deep ecology but challenges notions of dualistic relationships (such as *man/nature,* and therefore *man/woman, Western world/third world, black/white*) and critiques the extent to which masculine and racial bias colors that ecological theory (Shiva, 1989; Zimmerman, 1994). *Feminist environmental philosophy* begins with the recognition of male domination as the key to every expression of a patriarchal, hierarchical culture that produces exploitative practices toward women, non-Western and marginalized peoples, and nature (Cuomo, 1998; Plumwood, 1993).

Social ecology explores the cultural characteristics and patterns of social organizations and how they have contributed to the ecological crisis. It explains the ecological crisis as the result of authoritarian social structures, embodied most perniciously in capitalism but also present in state socialism (Zimmerman, 1994). Finally, *environmental sustainability* offers a tenuous reconciliation between the drive for perpetual economic growth with the realization that if development continues on its present trajectory, ecological disaster will ensue (Schrecker, 1997). The vision of sustainability is that humanity can learn to live in a relationship of harmony with the natural world. See Sumner (this volume) for a discussion of community sustainability.

This discussion of ecological theories describes radical approaches to environmentalism in that they critique and rewrite our notions of relationships within nature and with each other. Environmentalists subscribing to sustainable development see recovery as attainable through the integration of economic wants with environmental and social needs through nondegrading forms of agriculture and industry (Merchant, 1996). Deep ecology, social ecology, and ecological feminism emphasize (1) critical self-reflection, (2) a critique of normative institutions in Western cultures, (3) innovative approaches to interdisciplinary scholarship, and (4) experiential learning about *ecological identity*—our cognitive, affective, and intuitive perceptions of ecological relationships (Thomashow, 1995). Each of these approaches to ecology provides philosophical and practical frameworks with which to guide action.

Cultural Metaphors: Conceptions of Nature Reflected in Language

We unwittingly reveal our beliefs about the world and our place in it by the metaphors and figures of speech we use. The subconscious meanings we give to such terms as "humans," "wilderness," and "nature" tend to set us apart when humans are routinely described as "other" than nature. Language meanings are socially constructed and develop diverse representations of the "other"—particularly "women," "people of color," "third world," and "nature." Language has been successfully used to exclude people and maintain power, and therefore language use can expose attitudes of alienation, separation, and dominance.

Metaphors reveal how our thinking is ordered; they are the essence of thought, reason, and emotion. Mental images, including myths and metaphors, are more influential in how we see and act in the world than pure logic alone (Eisenberg, 1998). When aspects of a particular metaphor are valued, personally and culturally, they take on the moral significance of truth and can serve to influence goals and direct actions (Lakoff and Johnson, 1980). In North American society, for example, commonly shared cultural assumptions lead to perceiving change as social progress, viewing the environment from a human perspective, and representing the human as the basic social unit responsible for establishing the authority of ideas and values (Bowers, 1997).

Metaphors also serve to organize our worldview. A worldview equips a person with an understanding of the world, especially the relationships of different aspects of the world to each other (McKenzie, 1991). Worldviews are rooted in and shared within the cultural environment. An excellent example is *Pula,* the name of the currency of Botswana. Pula also means rain, and since the damming of the Zambezi River has caused drought in much of southern Africa, this evocative name reveals how precious both rain and other resources have become. Worldviews and their embedded metaphors can become dysfunctional—as are many currently in favor, such as *development* and *progress.* A pertinent example of a dysfunctional metaphor is *growth,* an honorific word in modern society. We are told we *should* be growing in economic output, in population, and in wealth, prestige, stature, and complexity. This has been taken to its extreme in globalization.

Ratinoff (1995) refers to globalization as a complex and major watershed in history. He feels it is a crisis because we are unable to perceive the new organizing principles behind the apparent disintegration of institutions and value systems. "Our habits of attention work against seeing, and the connections in the system are invisible" (Bateson, 1994, p. 138). "Each of us, with or without awareness, has the ability to connect to the whole interdependent web of life. . . . but most of us still seem to act as if the earth and its nonhuman aspects were separate from us, something 'out there' with no life of its own, and therefore unrelated to our 'merely personal' concerns (Conn, 1995, p. 157). Mack (1995) refers to this as species arrogance, a "psychology, or at least a prevailing attitude, conscious or unconscious, toward the earth. We regard it as a thing . . . to be owned, mined, fenced, guarded, stripped, built upon, dammed, plowed, burned, blasted, bulldozed, and melted to serve the material needs and desires of the human species at the expense, if necessary, of all other species (p. 282).

It is clear that the environment cannot withstand continued intensive demands for resources and the resulting "waste" disposal that a global economy is imposing. Wilber (2000) maintains that the "present environmental crisis is due primarily to a *fractured worldview* . . . that drastically separates mind and body, subject and object, culture and nature, thoughts and things, values and facts, spirit and matter, human and nonhuman; a worldview that is dualistic, mechanistic, atomistic, anthropocentric, and pathologically hierarchical" (p. 12, emphasis in original). It erroneously separates and improperly elevates humans above physical reality, and alienates humans from life, the earth, and the cosmos. Working to reveal and revise cultural notions of worldview can serve to facilitate social change and environmental action.

O'Sullivan (1999) developed the concept of "ecozoic consciousness that links ecology, social justice, and spirituality" (p. 2). This vision calls for a transformative restructuring of educational institutions at all levels that will enlarge our viewpoint beyond the marketplace to the planet and all creatures. Adult education must provide education that serves to counteract the dominant metaphor of irresponsible economic growth and assists people to reconnect with and value their natural environment. Thomashow (1995) writes that "as people widen their circles of identification, they become involved in thinking about the commons, the aspects of nature that everyone shares, and typically, this leads to participation in the public arena" (p. 3). While not everyone will choose to act, people can be supported in developing a greater sense of involvement in their community, a sense of shared identity, and to value interconnection. Carter (1992) writes that the search for a more adequate context of understanding leads to a comprehension of self that is inextricably linked with others, the earth, and the cosmos.

Metaphors in Adult Education Classrooms

Reflecting on the effects of the language choices we make as adult educators is perhaps a deceptively simple yet the most transformative action to undertake. Clover, Follen, and Hall (2000) state that environmental adult education is environmental in two respects: its content and its methods and means of communicating. The language and metaphors we choose make us teachers of sustainable development—or unsustainable development; educators of ecological understanding and peace with and in the natural world—or educators of violence against nature. If our language is devoid of nature, or unwittingly antinature, we need to question what worldview we might be inadvertently teaching. We can learn from the feminist movement, which has brought attention to and challenges the use of language that demeans and excludes women; and also from ecological feminism, which challenges language that equates women and marginalized people with a concept of nature separate from man (sic) that exists to be dominated, exploited, and oppressed (Plumwood, 1993; Shiva, 1989).

Lake (2001) suggests we should pay more attention to the emotional links in the language we employ. "The words we use *do* matter; they shape the way we look at the world" (p. 56). The use of language with negative connotations for "positive concepts creates a cognitive confusion that I believe has resulted in more muted support for the political and social actions that are needed" to address social and environmental injustice (p. 56). Some common phrases and metaphors seem innocuous, but upon reflection they are inimical to life. Using expressions like "killing two birds with one stone" creates subconscious images of violence toward nature. Why not use the more benign "healing two ailments with one remedy?" Likewise, discussion of a "dog-eat-dog world" or describing life as a "rat race" inaccurately characterizes the world as inherently competitive. Scientific discoveries of recent years have revealed a more cooperative, self-organizing natural world than was previously imagined, a world that is fundamentally interdependent (Capra, 1996; Karpiak, 2000). Unfortunately, this is not yet reflected in common language or worldviews.

When we unthinkingly choose metaphors of war, dominance, and oppression so commonplace in Western society, the incongruence of the disturbing associations can overshadow and detract from the positive content we hope to communicate. Working to change our ways of speech to reflect our values is a conscious act requiring sustained effort. We can learn to be aware of how frequently we use dysfunctional metaphors in our teaching, and whether we communicate the messages we would choose. The way we think and feel about the natural world is visible in our language, in our actions, and in much of the teaching we do. No matter the origins and familiarity of commonly used metaphors, we can learn to avoid those that perpetuate a destructive and exploitative antinature attitude. Our talk is in part our action.

Spirituality and the Environment

Metaphors and language are intimately connected with and express our spirituality. Moore (1994) lists some of the emotional complaints of our time, including feelings of emptiness, depression, loneliness, loss of values, and hungering for spirituality, and states his belief that these reflect a loss of soul. Our loneliness comes from an estrangement with a world depersonalized by our philosophies and worldviews, a world that is rendered dead in its essence. It is now impossible to remain unaware of the "pain of the Earth," as, according to Conn (1995), "we experience it physically, psychologically, economically or politically" (p. 161). Moore (1994) refers to ecology not as earth science, but as home science in recognition that "this world is our home and that our responsibility to it comes not from obligation or logic but from true affection" (p. 271).

Emerging expressions of spirituality focus on the interconnections of humans in nature and an appreciation for the divine in nature (Plaskow and Christ, 1989). When people are constantly required to change in response to the demands of the global economy, their needs for spiritual strength intensifies. The loneliness that feeds this yearning stems primarily from feeling disconnected from the natural world and denial that humans are an integral part of a world that is now in severe distress. Taking responsibility for preservation and restoration of the earth's health and integrity is a spiritual act that rejuvenates our full humanity. It is "time to fully heal this wound in human life—to find peace in our inner wildness and discover our deep kinship with the natural order" (Moore, 2002, p. 187).

In addressing spirituality within adult education, English and Gillen (2000) define spirituality as "awareness of something greater than ourselves, a sense that we are connected to all human beings and to all of creation" (p. 1). Just as Orr (1992) reminds us that all education is environmental education, Vella (2000) instructs that each "learning event is a moment of spiritual development" (p. 8). Addressing spirituality in our adult education practice means bringing our whole selves—mind, heart, and spirit—to our work and creating a learning space where learners can do the same. This can be a site for truly transformative learning, learning in which a deep inner shift in the meanings we hold of ourselves and our relationships within the world can take place (O'Sullivan, 1999). The goodness of spirit can heal our self-inflicted wounds (Wilber, 2000).

When we feel called to work for justice and peace, we are expressing our integrity as human beings and inviting others to do the same. It is a movement toward truth and authenticity. This is a spirituality of meaning, purpose, and motivation (English, 2003). Realizing what must change to create an ethical, interdependent, and healthy society is not enough—we are called to action. For many, the meaning of our lives and work for social and environmental justice are interconnected. Commitment and work, paid or not, are not separate, but can be intertwined within a person's life journey (Daloz, Keen, Keen, and Parks, 1996; Kovan and Dirkx, 2003; Tisdell, 2000).

To "critique the cultural myths that oppress us," we have to "have a conversation with the pain of our gut," and allow students the same privilege (O'Reilly, 1998, p. 34). All learners need support when experiencing the dissonance between our personal beliefs and those imparted by the dominant culture. This is courageous and difficult internal work for students and ourselves. When people come together to learn they can share mutual support for the journey. It is vital work because we must never forget that reconnecting with spirituality means survival of the earth's life forces and its beings.

As educators, we have responsibilities for forging a broad educational belief system that involves the cultivation of awe and wonder of the earth, assisting students in their process of meaning making, creation of metaphors and worldviews that nourish our capacity to live with and in the world, development of attitudes that allow us to act on wrongs we see in the world, and the ability to act responsibly on issues of justice and equity, and the celebration of diversity (O'Sullivan, 1999). An understanding of how spirituality is informed by culture, and how students' meaning-making efforts are informed by spirituality, helps educators create educational experiences that are more culturally relevant and truly transformative (Tisdell, 2003). As educators, we may be supporting a transformative learning journey of integration and a healing of separations between what we know and the dysfunctional myths and metaphors taught by society.

Environmental Adult Education

In writing of holistic thinking and education, Miller (1999) states that it "makes no sense to have spirituality without democracy, without social justice; without the healing of hatred and racial and class oppression; without a sustainable and nourishing relationship to the biosphere" (p. 195). In proposing spiritual principles to create a more sustainable, equitable world and linking these with adult education and community development practice, Bean (2000) begins with the requirement for an *ecological base* in recognition that humans are "one species within a complex, interdependent web of life" (p. 72) and follows with social justice, recognition of the dignity of the human person, working within a community base, action for liberation, and lastly combined reflection and action. Bringing concern for the environment into our teaching practices and learning theories offers the ability to address critical concerns that we and our students bring to our classrooms and work.

Many adults are working for social change amid the locus of challenging systems of oppression based on race, class, gender, and culture. Severe environmental degradation is intertwined with these as it occurs as an inherent part of that oppression. Race, class, gender, and the natural environment are often considered as separate sites of domination, but they are "systematically related. . . . Patterns of domination are integral to one another and work together in intricate patterns of oppression" (O'Sullivan, 1999, p. 160).

Energy for the struggle against oppressions based on race, class, and gender must never be diminished; however, these cannot be adequately acted against or theorized without acknowledging the inequitable impact of environmental problems. Much as when opposition to oppression began to be expressed in society and within adult education, environmental activism is being met with hostility and sometimes viewed as extraneous. Nevertheless, failure to address the environment in our teaching practice and literature is a serious omission.

Mitigating this requires changing our teaching, integrating concern for the environment in our learning theories, searching for relevant literature, and creating that literature when it cannot be found. Tompkins (1990) reassures us that we truly do have the power to make a difference, to create peace and justice and a more loving world, by the choices we make as adult educators. The learning environment is "a microcosm of the world; it is the chance we have to practice whatever ideals we may cherish. The kind of environment one creates is the acid test of what it is that one really stands for" (p. 656). Adult educators can provide leadership for change (Vaill, 1998). Our teaching reveals our politics. No matter the ideals we express, it is our words, actions, and interactions with students that convey who we are and what we believe.

Minding our metaphors and language is an important and vital first step. So is taking our teaching outdoors and inviting nature in. Creating opportunities for students to explore environmental issues of concern to them and relating them to their lives and the adult education literature can encourage them to critically engage with that literature and formulate a response to what they believe. Creating a teaching practice in which concerns for spirituality and the environment are accepted and valued for discussion is essential. Teaching this way means using a theory of engagement with the world and developing a quietness of mind that allows others to share their journeys. We can connect our spiritual beliefs to a sense of interconnection with others, compassion, global citizenship, and social action. We can learn to contribute to healing the self-created rift between ourselves and the rest of nature.

References

Bateson, M. C. *Peripheral Visions: Learning Along the Way.* New York: HarperCollins, 1994.

Bean, W. E. "Community Development and Adult Education: Locating Practice Within Its Roots." In L. M. English and M. A. Gillen (eds.), *Addressing the Spiritual Dimensions of Adult Learning: What Educators Can Do.* New Directions for Adult and Continuing Education, no. 85. San Francisco: Jossey-Bass, 2000.

Bowers, C. A. *The Culture of Denial: Why the Environmental Movement Needs a Strategy for Reforming Universities and Public Schools.* Albany: State University of New York Press, 1997.

Capra, F. *The Web of Life: A New Scientific Understanding of Living Systems.* New York: Anchor Books, 1996.

Carter, R. E. *Becoming Bamboo: Western and Eastern Explorations of the Meaning of Life.* Montreal/Kingston: McGill/Queen's University Press, 1992.

Clover, D. E., Follen, S., and Hall, B. *The Nature of Transformation: Environmental Adult Education.* (2nd ed.) Toronto: University of Toronto Press, 2000.

Conn, S. A. "When the Earth Hurts, Who Responds?" In T. Roszak, M. E. Gomes, and A. D. Kanner (eds.), *Ecopsychology: Restoring the Earth, Healing the Mind.* San Francisco: Sierra Club Books, 1995.

Cronon, W. (ed.). *Uncommon Ground: Rethinking the Human Place in Nature.* New York: Norton, 1996.

Cuomo, C. J. *Feminism and Ecological Communities: An Ethic of Flourishing.* London: Routledge, 1998.

Daloz, L. A., Keen, C. H., Keen, J. P., and Parks, S. D. *Common Fire: Leading Lives of Commitment in a Complex World.* Boston: Beacon Press, 1996.

Di Chiro, G. "Nature as Community: The Convergence of Environment and Social Justice." In W. Cronon (ed.), *Uncommon Ground: Rethinking the Human Place in Nature.* New York: Norton, 1996.

Eisenberg, E. *The Ecology of Eden: An Inquiry into the Dream of Paradise and a New Vision of Our Role in Nature.* New York: Vintage Books, 1998.

English, L. M. "Reclaiming Our Roots: Spirituality as an Integral Part of Adult Learning." *Adult Learning,* 2003, 12(3).

English, L. M., and Gillen, M. A. (eds.). *Addressing the Spiritual Dimensions of Adult Learning: What Educators Can Do.* New Directions for Adult and Continuing Education, no. 85. San Francisco: Jossey-Bass, 2000.

Karpiak, I. E. "Evolutionary Theory and the 'New Sciences': Rekindling Our Imagination for Transformation." *Studies in Continuing Education,* 2000, 22(1), 29–44.

Kovan, J. T., and Dirkx, J. M. "'Being Called Awake': The Role of Transformative Learning in the Lives of Environmental Activists." *Adult Education Quarterly,* 2003, 53(2), 99–118.

Lake, D. C. "Waging the War of the Worlds: Global Warming or Heating?" *Canadian Journal of Environmental Adult Education,* 2001, 6, 52–57.

Lakoff, G., and Johnson, M. *Metaphors We Live By.* Chicago: University of Chicago Press, 1980.

Mack, J. E. "The Politics of Species Arrogance." In T. Roszak, M. E. Gomes, and A. D. Kanner (eds.), *Ecopsychology: Restoring the Earth, Healing the Mind.* San Francisco: Sierra Club Books, 1995.

McKenzie, L. *Adult Education and Worldview Construction.* Malabar, Fla.: Krieger, 1991.

Merchant, C. "Reinventing Eden: Western Culture as a Recovery Narrative." In W. Cronon (ed.), *Uncommon Ground: Rethinking the Human Place in Nature.* New York: Norton, 1996.

Miller, R. "Holistic Education for an Emerging Culture." In S. Glazer (ed.), *The Heart of Learning: Spirituality in Education.* Los Angeles: Tarcher, 1999.

Moore, T. *Care of the Soul: A Guide for Cultivating Depth and Sacredness in Everyday Life.* San Francisco: HarperCollins, 1994.

Moore, T. *The Soul's Religion: Cultivating a Profoundly Spiritual Way of Life.* New York: HarperCollins, 2002.

O'Reilly, M. R. *Radical Presence: Teaching as Contemplative Practice.* Portsmouth, N.H.: Boynton/Cook, 1998.

Orr, D. W., *Ecological Literacy:* Education and the Transition to a Postmodern World. Albany: State University of New York Press, 1992.

O'Sullivan, E. *Transformative Learning: Education Vision for the 21st Century.* London: Zed Books, 1999.

Plaskow, J., and Christ, C. O. *Weaving the Visions: New Patterns in Feminist Spirituality.* San Francisco: HarperCollins, 1989.

Plumwood, V. *Feminism and the Mastery of Nature.* New York: Routledge, 1993.

Ratinoff, L. "Global Insecurity and Education: The Culture of Globalization." *Prospects,* 1995, 25(2), 147–174.

Schrecker, T. *Surviving Globalism: The Social and Environmental Challenges.* New York: St. Martin's Press, 1997.

Shiva, V. *Staying Alive: Women, Ecology and Development.* London: Zed Books, 1989.

Thomashow, M. *Ecological Identity: Becoming a Reflective Environmentalist.* Cambridge, Mass.: MIT Press, 1995.

Tisdell, E. J. "Spirituality and Emancipatory Adult Education in Women Adult Educators Working for Social Justice." *Adult Education Quarterly,* 2000, 50(4), 308–335.

Tisdell, E. J. *Exploring Spirituality and Culture in Adult and Higher Education.* San Francisco: Jossey-Bass, 2003.

Tompkins, J. "Pedagogy of the Distressed." *College English,* 1990, 52(6), 653–660.

Vaill, P. *Spirited Leading and Learning: Process Wisdom for a New Age.* San Francisco: Jossey-Bass, 1998.

Vella, J. "A Spirited Epistemology: Honoring the Adult Learner as Subject." In L. M. English and M. A. Gillen (eds.), *Addressing the Spiritual Dimensions of Adult Learning: What Educators Can Do.* New Directions for Adult and Continuing Education, no. 85. San Francisco: Jossey-Bass, 2000.

Welton, M. "Social Revolutionary Learning: The New Social Movements as Learning Sites." *Adult Education Quarterly,* 1993, 43(3), 152–164.

Wilber, K. *Sex, Ecology, Spirituality: The Spirit of Evolution.* (2nd ed., revised) Boston: Shambala Publications, 2000.

Zimmerman, M. E. *Contesting Earth's Future: Radical Ecology and Postmodernism.* Berkeley: University of California Press, 1994.

LILIAN H. HILL *is education specialist and assistant professor at Virginia Commonwealth University in Richmond, Virginia.*

JULIE D. JOHNSTON *is a teacher educator and environmental adult educator in British Columbia, Canada.*

3

Environmental adult education contributes to environmental justice learning by mobilizing citizen participation, popular activism, and direct action which are essential for democracy and for healthy people and ecosystems.

Environmental Justice: Environmental Adult Education at the Confluence of Oppressions

Robert J. Hill

Environmental justice (EJ) refers to the principle of equitable protection from environmental hazards for all races, ethnicities, and socioeconomic groups, and preservation of natural resources of the people, including indigenous communities (Sexton and Anderson, 1993; Toxics Watch, 1995). It emerged as a new social movement in the late 1960s in the United States through such initiatives as the United Church of Christ Commission for Racial Justice's adult religious education enterprise (1987), which had a galvanizing effect on the movement (Novotny, 2000). Other important components were the farm worker campaigns in California, Texas, and Florida; Chicano organizing in New Mexico; indigenous peoples resisting mercury contamination of their tribal waters, resource extraction on sacred lands, uranium contamination, and the targeting of territory for toxic and nuclear waste; and women confederating to educate, mobilize, and confront toxic exposure of their neighborhoods and families ("Summary of Accomplishments," 2002).

In more than three decades, the EJ movement has built national and international, multiracial and multiethnic communities of knowledge. It has witnessed two summits—the first and the second summits of the National People of Color Environmental Leadership (held in Washington, D.C., in 1991 and 2002). Movement members have assumed leadership roles at both the U.N. Conference on Environment and Development—the Earth Summit that produced and adopted Agenda 21, a program for sustainable development (held in Rio de Janeiro in 1992) and the World Sum-

NEW DIRECTIONS FOR ADULT AND CONTINUING EDUCATION, no. 99, Fall 2003 © Wiley Periodicals, Inc.

mit on Sustainable Development (held in Johannesburg, 2002). It has spawned a number of submovements, such as the global climate justice movement, which posits that the effects of extreme weather events due to pollution disproportionately burden those contributing the least to climate change. The movement has witnessed seismic shifts to include voter rights and refugee concerns to its ecological agenda. Since 1990, it has struggled with national and international mainstream environmental organizations over patterns of environmental racism within them. In 2002, at the Second National People of Color Environmental Leadership Summit, efforts were made to craft "Principles of Collaboration" to ensure alliance-building and consultation between local EJ community groups and larger mainstream organizations. Paradoxically, as the EJ movement has matured, it has become more populated by energetic and visionary youth and student components with a broad social agenda and holistic view of EJ that includes rights for lesbians, gay men, bisexuals, transgendered and queer people, and global peace for all.

What's in a Name?

Variously named *ecological justice, ecojustice,* and *environmental equity,* the movement is larger than the construction known as *environmental racism,* which, during testimony to the U.S. Subcommittee on Civil and Constitutional Rights in 1993, Bullard described as policies, practices, or directives that differentially affect or disadvantage—intentionally or otherwise—individuals, groups, or communities based on race or color. *Environmental equity,* the moniker coined by the U.S. Environmental Protection Agency (EPA), is based on the concept of distributive justice; that is, that all social groups should be equally protected. The term has drawn criticism as a way for the state to domesticate the discourse, to deny the reality of race bias, and for suggesting that equally shared exposure to contamination is tolerable.

Environmental justice has become an academic field of study that takes into account the dynamics of inequality originating in social, political, and environmental attitudes, behaviors, actions, decision making, and policies. It explores disparities at the intersections of class, race, ethnicity, and gender at the global, international, hemispheric, national, regional, and local levels on issues related to the just distributions of natural resources, protection of the natural world, and sharing of environmental burdens. The confluence of such cultural practices as racism, white privilege, sexism, greed, and class advantage become especially dangerous intersections for many people when measured in environmental terms. Environmental adult education takes up activist projects, community building and solidarity, resistance, and marshaling networks of knowledge to reverse the hazardous impacts of this confluence of oppressions.

Environmental justice (EJ) includes education to assist adults in remedying the disproportionate burden carried by low-income communities and people of color related to a series of global events and processes. These embrace the unhealthy consequences of extraction and exploitation of natural resources in developing countries by overprivileged, technologically developed nations; increased probability of exposure to environmental hazards; global climate change; and release of toxic wastes and poisonous dumping. EJ education also centers on cities, for example, by challenging urban sprawl; the spatial layout of central cities and suburbs; differential delivery of environmental services like household waste removal; urban air quality; metal poisoning of poor children, often from lead paint in old housing stock; unequal economic development; and disparate access to or insufficient maintenance of natural resource amenities such as green space, parks, and playgrounds. Agriculture also is intersected by environmental adult education, such as the focus on waning rights to food and food security; the impact of genetically modified foods; and exposure of agricultural laborers to pesticides. Facility siting is another great concern to EJ educators; it covers the uneven placement of energy plants, hazardous waste treatment units, nuclear test sites, and nuclear disposal areas. Minorities also carry the burden of pollution associated with the manufacture, storage, and transport of toxic materials. Labor becomes involved in environmental justice education related to inadequate worker occupational safety from chemicals. The effects of unequal application of environmental processes and policies, and differential enforcement of environmental regulations, such as tardiness or inaction against environmental violators, and meager fines for environmental criminals who pollute communities where the poor and people of color reside, are signals of environmental injustice and are triggers for education.

Environmental popular education is a key element in the EJ movement. This form of adult education most often takes place where there are environmental dilemmas. It is rooted in firsthand experiences of the people and results in the local creation of meaning with the aim of transforming unacceptable conditions in people's lives.

As a global phenomenon, examples of environmental adult and popular education can be gathered from the southeastern United States (Bullard, 1990, 2000) to South Africa (Lengwati, 1995), Central Mexico (Oliver, 2000) and to the South Pacific (Guevara, 2000). Environmental adult education is readily illustrated in popular activism and indigenous agency in India (Kapoor, 2000), where popular education is used to encourage indigenous peoples to assert themselves to protect their culture, to reconfigure power in indigenous-state relations, and to protect the environment. Environmental popular education encourages community organizing to remedy fragmentation and dehumanization that occur for many reasons and that foster injustice, including poverty, illiteracy, landlessness, joblessness, dependency on land owners, lack of community development facilities, and racial division. Organizing at grassroots levels can present remedies through nonformal adult education offered by and to people who are local to various problems.

Environmental Adult and Popular Education: Continuing the Social Justice Tradition

The field of adult education has a long and respected history in learning related to social problems and societal transformation. In the early part of this century, E. C. Lindeman and J. Dewey advocated action to stimulate social engagement and to foster change (Heaney, 1996). Examples of adult education theory, research, and practice with a social agenda that includes justice, equality, democracy, and civil liberties are considerable (Cunningham, 1988; Hart, 1990). Recently, adult education for environmental justice has emerged as a new focus (Finger and Asun, 2000; Newman, 1996). Moema Viezzer (1992) suggests that adult education should support the fundamental liberties of life, including "the right to breathe clean air, to eat nontoxic foods, to live without radioactivity from the effects of nuclear disasters, and to be free from manipulations caused by the developments of bio-technology and genetic engineering" (p. 7). Hill (1997) recommends that environmental adult education gain the skills necessary to negotiate the terrain of the everyday life-world in an environmentally sensitive way. His call is for adult education to play a primary role in building environmental democracies. This is achieved through principles of environmental protection, human rights, social justice, participatory decision making, and active citizenship.

Grassroots Movement Learning and Public Policy: Creating Environmental Justice on a Global Scale

Social movements, including the EJ movement, are sites of much adult learning, meaning making, and resistance (Finger, 1989; Habermas, 1981; Welton, 1993). They also challenge and democratize power that has become concentrated in the "system world" (Kapoor, 2000). The United States alone has an estimated seven thousand grassroots groups of citizens engaged in community development through implicit or explicit educational efforts, for protection from pollution or to preserve natural resources (Miller, 1992). An undetermined number of self-organized, action-oriented, problem-solving groups abound globally. For most of these collectives, the purpose of joining together is not only for adult education, study, or discussion but also for education directed at action. Entities active in EJ adult education for social change include community-based Green political parties, labor and trade unions, workers' associations, farmers' associations, community-supported agriculture and food cooperatives, artisan and professional groups, guilds, community housing, health care workers, socially active religious and spiritual movement members, artists, writers, filmmakers, videographers, rappers, and folk and rock musicians. Currently these groups bring hope to civil society and its democratic and ecological project (Morrison, 1995).

Environmental justice proponents often arise from previously existing organizational and institutional networks that are sites of prior adult learning. In the United States these include historically black colleges and universities, churches, faith-based communities, and neighborhood improvement associations (Sandweiss, 1998) and provide opportunities for action on specific local environmental situations (Camacho, 1998). Additionally, different sectors of the larger social justice movement, with formerly unacknowledged lines of common linkage, are converging. Thus, members of the antiwar movement articulate the environmental costs of war (Wall, 2001) and the disproportionate impact it has on minority communities.

The implications are unequivocal: the further vested people are in any aggrieved community, the more likely they are to mobilize. As adults, they are at significant moments positioned to engage in EJ learning. Participants in EJ learning often subscribe to the notions of Ibikunle-Johnson (1989) that serious environmental problems seen today are a result of wrong management decisions, a lack of education and training, and inadequate or erroneous information.

Significant change in society often comes from the bottom up rather than from the top down (Miller, 1992). Morrison (1995) demonstrates that reform from above does not engender democracy, but instead democracy is created by insistent action from below. To him, ecological democracy arises from popular ferment, hope for a better life, intolerance of the abuse of power, and collective and personal determination to build equitable lifeworlds. Education for ecological democracy must begin with growth and empowerment of community-based associations that are the heart of civil society. It is within these associations that knowledge is constructed and new meaning is possible.

While mainstream environmental education may potentially play a significant role in building ecological democracy, its actual reproduction of social inequality often stands in the way. Novotny (2000) found that the rubric of normative environmental education could not be untangled from the ideology of liberal culture where, for instance, expanding the curriculum is positioned as a substitute for the unpleasantness of political struggle, and a new reading list stands in for social change.

The Power of Economic Discourses

Adult educators face a daunting task of building an environmental democracy and a class of ecologically knowledgeable citizens in capitalist societies that construct "economic discourse" as naturally given, nonpolitical, and beyond critique (Nash, 2000). The privileging of economic discourse advantages corporations and industries, some of which are in the forefront of environmental pillage. Additionally, communities predisposed to environmental injustice due to their socioeconomic status, lack of access to power, and level of literacy are often faced with "blackmail" that forces them to accept financial incentives extended by industry and commerce over pressing problems of systematic pollution or resource depletion (Lester, Allen, and Hill, 2001).

Since social consensus is largely a function of social position and power, the market has been successful with its own "other" environmental education, sometimes characterized as "anti-environmental" (Hill, 2002). Conservatives, including those in the market sector, resist public participation by a populace they perceive as uninformed or ill-informed, calling public participation "system overload" (King, 1975).

The market sector has allies in both the academy and in government contesting the growing consensus that people of color, indigenous communities, and low-income communities are often treated as less valuable than people of the dominant culture. For example, in a paper published for Washington University's Center for the Study of American Business, Boerner and Lambert (1994) argue that, "despite a number of high-profile studies, the existing research does not substantiate environmental advocates' claims of discriminatory siting [of polluting facilities]" (p. 22). The authors warn U.S. policymakers not to fall prey to the persuasive arguments of environmental racism, and not to alter public policy through regulatory solutions.

Community-Driven Environmental Justice Education and Research: Confronting Knowledge Experts

Some of the most important contributions of EJ movement learning surround the nature of science, the role of knowledge experts (canonists) in environmental decision making, and a fundamental critique of science itself. While EJ educator/activists may employ canonical information produced by knowledge specialists, they also recognize that local people have valuable knowledge. As a result, many activists challenge the scientific establishment (Merrifield, 1989), especially when it rejects lay-expert opinion. Grassroots education commonly contests scientific truth-claims and attempts to renegotiate power asymmetries when personal experiences conflict with "official" understandings of environmental scenarios. In challenging scientific ways of knowing, activist/educators accept experiential knowledge that experts usually dismiss. They show that allegedly detached scientific inquiry actually has hidden political agendas. Activist educators trouble the notions that research design, specific sampling techniques, and data-gathering procedures are required for "knowing." They recognize that controlled measurement of outcomes and the development of causal models with predictive power are privileged ways of making meaning. The environmental justice movement challenges the demands of professional experts for absolute certainty, statistical significance, and empirical assurance before action is undertaken. The movement exposes the cultural politics of scientific knowledge.

EJ participatory research proposes to replace the supremacy of empirical, techno-rational ways of meaning making. People of color and poor communities in the EJ movement provide clear examples of the social and cultural foundations of knowledge. This is powerfully illustrated by the participatory action research done at Highlander Education and Research Center. This Center is a model of organizing, community education, and community development in the southeastern region of the United States and contributes to efforts for global change (*Environment and Development in the USA*, n.d.; Israel and others, 1991).

Education for Environmental Justice: A Response to Globalization

Globalization is a contemporary term that points to multiple and drastic changes occurring in all arenas of social life, but especially in economics and culture (Stromquist and Monkman, 2000). Globalization processes have generated considerable concern within the environmental justice movement. Many of the institutions and apparatuses of globalization, including transnational corporations and multilateral financial groups such as the World Bank (WB), the International Monetary Fund (IMF), and the World Trade Organization (WTO) have been accused of fostering ecologically and socially destructive development in less technologically developed countries. As a result, adult education as activism and resistance has focused on these and numerous other perpetrators of globalization.

Environmental justice education is employed in several ways in the debate on globalization, including to increase people's awareness of the impacts of globalization on everyday life, and to highlight ways to remediate the negative impacts of globalization on education itself (Stromquist, 2002). Protest and direct action at gatherings of global capitalists have given momentum to environmental justice learning. Educational content focuses on central governments' and transnational corporations' disinterest in preserving the fragile relationships between humans and the natural world; the growing inequality between haves and have-nots both *within* rich nation-states and *between* lender-states and states in debt to them; the asymmetry of political and economic power; cultural homogenization; overutilization of the world's resources by an elite group of consumers; genetic engineering; and the impact of turbocapitalism—excesses carried out by techno-organizational change and the free market, through private enterprise that has become uncoupled from government regulations. (See Finger and Asun, 2000, for a discussion of the impacts of unbridled capitalism on the earth's resources.)

Learning opportunities, especially those fostered through environmental popular education by nongovernmental agencies (NGOs) and other sectors of civil society, take many forms, including community art (Clover, 2000); teach-ins and campus organizing; dedicated days for conscientization (such as Earth Day, International Workers Day, and the International Day Against Consumption); direct action and public protest (numerous recent antiglobalization events that offered massive education and direct-action training); religious and ethics education activities (for example, Jubilee Movement International, an effort to lift nations and their peoples out of foreign debt bondage); educational activities conducted by labor unions; humor and creativity (for example, the Raging Grannies, cultural icons in Canada [Roy, 2000]); and grassroots activities of aboriginal peoples, indigenous communities, and women.

Conclusions: Learning from the Dangerous Intersections of Class, Race, Ethnicity, and Gender with the Environment

Michel Foucault (1980) wrote that new social movements develop in opposition to the effects of power that are linked to knowledge. Michael Newman (1999) states that social movements perform numerous functions, such as allowing people to oppose or bring about change, to foster collective action, to learn new skills, to examine values and assumptions about themselves and others, and to construct new meaning and understanding. People can learn to recognize structures of social control, to develop forms of action to exert or oppose power, to generate ideas not previously articulated, to take up personal growth strategies, and to create new kinds of knowledge. Many of these are accomplished through social movement learning that leads to social transformation and more equitable conditions for marginalized and low-income people, aboriginal communities, and people of color. Environmental adult education in popular movements is at the root of this change.

Globally, low-income families, women, indigenous peoples, oppressed communities, and communities of color have raised ecological consciousness, altered public policy, and in some instances transformed civil society. One mechanism for this has been to resignify the meaning of *distributive justice*. Environmental injustice is not solved by reallocating pollution from contaminated areas to more pristine ones or by greater sharing of natural resource exploitation between or among nations. Rather, it requires a reexamination of the reasons for pollution and despoliation of resources that fuel an elite class's voracious appetite for "progress" and "modernization." Grassroots activist/educators recognize the role they play in bringing about a new environmental citizenry that will engage in this type of inquiry.

Adult education within the EJ paradigm points to a redefinition of the term "environment"—which is no longer reduced to "nature." Ecojustice educators' efforts have inscribed new meaning to the term to include the environment of families and communities, and not merely "wilderness" and "nonhuman beings." They present a holistic view of the constructed, cultural, and natural environments as part of a political whole (Salazar, 1996), including economic structures and behaviors of people. Knowledge generated within the movement is informative, aimed at explanations; reflective, oriented toward better understanding of environmental problems; normative, aimed at making judgments and taking a position on how the world ought to be; and imperative/action-oriented, directed at agency along a continuum from letter writing to disruptive acts of massive civil disobedience.

Low-income communities—where people of color reside—aboriginal groups, and women have much to offer policymakers on the issue of public participation. They are committed to accountability and transparency in interactions between and among civil society, the state, and the market. They show that environmental science and politics can be democratized (Gottlieb, 1993). They open up solutions to problems beyond techno-rational responses. Robyn and Camacho (1998) postulate that we are in a state of environmental deterioration requiring alternative public policy approaches because current efforts simply are not working. The ecojustice movement offers fresh hope through new ways of being and doing in the world. Public policy based on EJ suggests that adult education for environmental democracy is appropriate for several reasons. It is more likely to represent the interests of future generations, to better fight the interests of unchecked capitalists, to assume activities on the local level where empowerment can occur, and to enable participation in both deliberation and decision-making processes (de-Shalit, 2000).

The impacts of EJ learning extend to a host of diverse arenas such as feminist discourse, participatory research, and the production of scientific knowledge. For example, Hynes (1999) extends the concerns of ecojustice to women, stating that the impeccable logic of environmental justice around the intersections of race and class is convincing for gender as well. Like racial justice, a sexual justice that seeks to eliminate the sexual exploitation of women is fundamental to environmental justice, to community health, and to social goodness (p. 201). Likewise, in part because of the EJ movement, concepts of science have changed from a neutral, nonpolitical, value-free, and benevolent enterprise that solves problems to the recognition that science can partially be the cause of problems (Merrifield, 1989). Alternative dimensions of EJ include citizens as local lay-experts and as popular epidemiologists, illustrating that positionality determines both what one observes and how one observes it.

A variety of solutions to EJ problems have been proposed through environmental adult and popular education. These include toxics use reduction (pollution prevention); improved participation in the public environmental decision-making process; improved access to environmental data and information; increased research on health risks caused by exposure to contaminants; and improved enforcement and compliance of laws, based on an increased sensitivity to environmental injustices embedded in rule making. These solutions suggest important roles for public research and educational institutions. Environmental justice discourse shows that, as part of the development of public issues education, adult educators engaged in environmental policy have a unique role to fulfill (Danielson, 2001). Data suggest that formal education may have less impact than education occurring in the nonformal sector. Universities and colleges routinely avoid dealing with social inequalities and public issues education (Novotny, 2000). This raises doubts about the role the academy can play in resolving EJ problems and highlights the necessity of grassroots environmental adult and popular education as a means to challenge and subvert racism, class privilege, and gender discrimination that are often the basis for environment injustice.

References

Boerner, C., and Lambert, T. *Environmental Justice?* Washington, D.C.: Washington University Center for the Study of American Business, Apr. 1994.

Bullard, R. D. "Environmentalism, Economic Blackmail, and Civil Rights: Competing Agendas Within the Black Community." In J. Gaventa, B. Smith, and A. Willingham (eds.), *Communities in Economic Crisis: Appalachia and the South.* Philadelphia: Temple University Press, 1990.

Bullard, R. D. *Dumping in Dixie: Race, Class and Environmental Quality.* Boulder, Colo.: Westview Press, 2000.

Camacho, D. E. "The Environmental Justice Framework: A Political Framework." In D. E. Camacho (ed.), *Environmental Injustices, Political Struggles: Race, Class, and the Environment.* Durham, N.C.: Duke University Press, 1998.

Clover, D. E. "Community Arts as Environmental Education and Activism." *Convergence,* 2000, *33*(3), 19–31.

Cunningham, P. M. "The Adult Educator and Social Responsibility." In R. G. Brockett (ed.), *Ethical Issues in Adult Education.* New York: Teachers College, 1988.

Danielson, L. E. "Economic Development, Health Risks and Concern for Environmental Justice." [http://www.ces.ncsu.edu/depts/agecon/PIE/ejsumm.html]. Aug. 18, 2001.

de-Shalit, A. *The Environment: Between Theory and Practice.* London: Oxford University Press, 2000.

Environment and Development in the USA: A Grassroots Report for UNCED. New Market, Tenn.: Community Environmental Health Program, Highlander Research and Education Center, n.d.

Finger, M. "New Social Movements and Their Implications for Adult Education." *Adult Education Quarterly,* 1989, *40*(1), 5–21.

Finger, M., and Asun, J. M. *Adult Education at the Crossroads: Learning Our Way Out.* London: Zed Books, 2000.

Foucault, M. *Power/Knowledge: Selected Interviews and Other Writings.* New York: Pantheon, 1980.

Gottlieb, R. *Forcing the Spring: The Transformation of the American Environmental Movement.* Washington, D.C.: Island Press, 1993.

Guevara, J. R. "Rethinking the Local-Global Links in Grassroots Environmental Education." *Convergence,* 2000, *33*(3), 74–85.

Habermas, J. "New Social Movements." *Telos,* 1981, *49*, 33–37.

Hart, M. "Critical Theory and Beyond: Further Perspectives on Emancipatory Education." *Adult Education Quarterly,* 1990, *40*(3), 125–138.

Heaney, T. *Adult Education for Social Change: From Center Stage to the Wings and Back Again.* Information Series, no. 365. Columbus, Ohio: ERIC Clearinghouse on Adult, Career, and Vocational Education, 1996. (ED 396 190)

Hill, R. J. "Growing Grassroots: Environmental Conflict, Adult Education and the Quest for Cultural Authority." Unpublished doctoral dissertation, Adult Education Program, Pennsylvania State University, 1997.

Hill, R. J. "Pulling Up Grassroots: A Study of the Right-Wing 'Popular' Adult Environmental Education Movement in the USA." *Studies in Continuing Education,* 2002, 24(2), 181–203.

Hynes, N. P. "Consumption: North American Perspectives." In J. Silliman and Y. King (eds.), *Dangerous Intersections: Feminist Perspectives on Population, Environment, and Development.* Boston: South End Press, 1999.

Ibikunle-Johnson, V. "Managing the Community's Environment: Grassroots Participation and Environmental Education." *Convergence,* 1989, 22(4), 13–23.

Israel, B., and others. *Environmental Activists Share Knowledge and Experiences: Description and Evaluation of STP Schools at the Highlander Research and Education Center.* CRSO (Center for Research on Social Organizations) Working Paper Series. (PCMA [Program on Conflict Management Alternatives] Working Paper no. 29). Ann Arbor, MI: University of Michigan, 1991.

Kapoor, D. "Environmental Popular Activism and Indigenous Activism in India." *Convergence,* 2000, 33(3), 32–43.

King, A. "Overload: The Problems of Governing in the 1970s." *Political Studies,* 1975, 23, 284–296.

Lengwati, D. M. "The Politics of Environmental Destruction and the Use of Nature as Teacher and Site of Learning." *Convergence,* 1995, 28(4), 99–103.

Lester, J. P., Allen, D. W., and Hill, K. M. *Environmental Injustice in the United States: Myths and Realities.* Boulder, Colo.: Westview Press, 2001.

Merrifield, J. *Putting Scientists in Their Place: Participatory Research in Environmental and Occupational Health.* Working Paper Series, no. 12. New Market, Tenn.: Economics Education Project, Highlander Research and Education Center, 1989.

Miller, G. T. *Living in the Environment: An Introduction to Environmental Science.* Belmont, Calif.: Wadsworth, 1992.

Morrison, R. *Ecological Democracy.* Boston: South End Press, 1995.

Nash, K. *Contemporary Political Sociology: Globalization, Politics, and Power.* Cambridge, Mass.: Blackwell, 2000.

Newman, M. *Defining the Enemy: Adult Education in Social Action.* Paddington, New South Wales: Stewart Victor, 1996.

Newman, M. *Maeler's Regard: Images of Adult Learning.* Sydney: Stewart Victor, 1999.

Novotny, P. *Where We Live, Work, and Play: The Environmental Justice Movement and the Struggle for a New Environmentalism.* New York: Praeger, 2000.

Oliver, B. "Participation in Environmental Popular Education Workshops: An Example from Mexico." *Convergence,* 2000, 33(3), 44–53.

Robyn, L., and Camacho, D. E. "Bishigendan akii: Respect the Earth." In D. E. Camacho (ed.), *Environmental Injustices, Political Struggles: Race, Class, and the Environment.* Durham, N.C.: Duke University Press, 1998.

Roy, C. "Raging Grannies and Environmental Issues: Humor and Creativity in Educative Protests." *Convergence,* 2000, 33(3), 6–17.

Salazar, D. *Environmental Justice: Grassroots Activists Push the Frontiers of Forestry and Politics.* William P. Thompson Memorial Lecture Series. Northern Arizona University, College of Ecosystem Science and Management, Apr. 10, 1996.

Sandweiss, S. "The Social Construction of Environmental Justice." In D. E. Camacho (ed.), *Environmental Injustices, Political Struggles: Race, Class, and the Environment.* Durham, N.C.: Duke University Press, 1998.

Sexton, K., and Anderson, Y. B. "Foreword." *Toxicology and Industrial Health,* 1993, 9(special issue 5), vi.

Stromquist, N. P. *Education in a Globalized World: The Connectivity of Power, Technology, and Knowledge.* Lanham, Md.: Rowman & Littlefield, 2002.

Stromquist, N. P., and Monkman, K. (eds.). *Globalization and Education: Integration and Contestation Across Cultures.* Lanham, Md.: Rowman & Littlefield, 2002.

"Summary of Accomplishments of the Environmental Justice Networks." Paper presented at the Second National People of Color Environmental Leadership Summit, Washington, D.C., Oct. 23, 2002.

Toxics Watch. "Environmental Justice." In *Toxics Watch 1995.* New York: INFORM, 1995.

United Church of Christ Commission for Racial Justice. *Toxic Wastes and Race in the United States: A National Report on the Racial and Socioeconomic Characteristics of Communities Surrounding Hazardous Waste Sites.* New York: United Church of Christ, 1987.

Viezzer, M. "Learning for Environmental Action." *Convergence,* 1992, 25(2), 3–8.

Wall, R. "War and the Environment: Some of the Ways that Military Actions Can Affect the Ecosystem." [http://www.acnatsci.org/research/kye/KYE22001.html]. Nov. 1, 2001.

Welton, M. "Social Revolutionary Learning: The New Social Movements as Learning Sites." *Adult Education Quarterly,* 1993, 43(3), 152–164.

ROBERT J. HILL *is assistant professor of adult education at the University of Georgia-Athens.*

*Local communities face many challenges in an increas-
ingly globalized world. A new framework for sustainability that includes environmental adult education can help
them survive, and even thrive, in the age of globalization.*

Environmental Adult Education and Community Sustainability

Jennifer Sumner

Community sustainability is an issue of local importance with global implications. Without viable, healthy communities, we lose the basis for understanding what humans need to live, work, and enjoy life to the fullest
capacity. Even in a globalized world, the concept of place is still vitally
important as an expression of our connection with each other and with the
environment.

Both rural and urban communities are increasingly challenged by
global forces over which they seem to have little control, but which affect
them in profoundly complex ways. How can they meet these challenges,
and still remain sustainable? One of the solutions involves learning new
ways of engaging with the world that prioritize the environment, support
community sustainability, and provide an inspiration to others who are also
facing global challenges.

Challenges to Community Sustainability

While communities around the world are feeling the impacts of global cultural, social, and political forces, by far the most overwhelming problems
come from the economic forces known as corporate globalization. This
process is driven by an economic agenda that promotes the rights of
transnational corporations over other sorts of rights, such as human rights,
women's rights, labor rights, indigenous rights, or environmental rights.
These corporate rights are promoted by policies that seek to lower corporate taxes and accommodate international flows of speculative capital, policies that seek to reduce public expenditures and privatize public services,

NEW DIRECTIONS FOR ADULT AND CONTINUING EDUCATION, no. 99, Fall 2003 © Wiley Periodicals, Inc.

and policies that seek to deregulate business and secure monopoly private property rights under law ("Globalism Project," 2001).

Rural and urban communities are the interface between people and policy, and the implications of such global policies play out at local levels. For example, international trade agreements that allow corporations to lay claim to future profits inhibit communities from penalizing pollution of local water sources for fear of being sued for loss of future profits by corporate polluters. It is little wonder that many communities feel impotent in the face of such global power. And as the gap between rich and poor increases exponentially under corporate globalization, those left behind—both individuals and communities—are excluded from the benefits these policies are claimed to promote. Such exclusion undermines urban and rural communities, leaving them vulnerable to fragmentation and collapse (Sumner, 2000) and challenging their sustainability.

These global corporate policies also negatively impact the environment that all communities depend on. Herman Daly (1999), former senior economist for the World Bank, argues that the environment cannot sustain the massive growth that corporate globalization entails. In essence, the environment is used as a source and a sink in the never-ending quest for increasing returns for corporate stockholders and senior management. Under this scenario of the global growth machine, "Our forests are overlogged, our agricultural lands overcropped, our grasslands overgrazed, our wetlands overdrained, our groundwaters overtapped, our seas overfished, and just about the whole terrestrial and marine environment overpolluted with chemical and radioactive poisons" (Goldsmith, 1997, p. 242).

Almost by definition, the growth entailed by corporate globalization results in environmental destruction. The environmental effects of the growth imperative can be seen in the so-called tiger economies of East Asia, where "air pollution in cities is growing faster than the rate of economic growth" (Redclift, 1999, p. 71). The growth imperative is also evident in the ecological degradation that accompanies corporate agriculture, which needs to "continually expand production to maintain profits" (Allen and Sachs, 1991, p. 575), decreasing environmental viability as it increases shareholder value. At the same time as we are experiencing this "environmental race to the bottom" (Brecher, Costello, and Smith, 2000, p. 11), the mechanisms for dealing with environmental problems have decreased in the current neoliberal climate of deregulation and lax enforcement. Ecologist Robert Ayres (cited in Ellwood, 2001) sums up the situation: "There is every indication that human economic activity supported by perverse trade and growth policies is well on the way to perturbing our natural environment more and faster than any known event in planetary history, save perhaps the large asteroid collision that may have killed off the dinosaurs. We may well be on the way to our own extinction" (p. 3).

In essence, protecting communities and the environment is now a barrier to international trade. Protectionism itself has become a dirty word, leaving both rural and urban communities, and the environment they depend on, without the support required for sustainability.

Challenges to Environmental Adult Education

The policies associated with corporate globalization affect not only communities and the environment but education as well. These policies include reduced public spending and privatization of all levels of education. Under this agenda, education is no longer a human right, but a commodity for sale to those who can afford it. The rise of educational management organizations (EMOs) are a symptom of this fundamental change in education. These organizations "contribute to a climate which pressures public institutions to reinvent themselves to reflect the needs of the marketplace— whereupon they can be offered an 'internationally proven' option, at enormous profit for themselves" (Shaker, 1999, p. vii).

In this cost-cutting and privatizing climate, adult education is changing. While many forms of adult education have their roots in social change, the field has become narrowed, and according to Griff Foley (2001, p. 80), "vocationalized"—providing labor market training through private agencies for the secondary labor force and the unemployed. In addition, in line with the policies of corporate globalization, government support is being withdrawn from adult education, with the profitable aspects being handed over to private concerns and the unprofitable aspects being downloaded to communities. In this corporate climate, "the very notion of 'adult education' is disappearing" (Foley, 2001, p. 84).

Environmental adult education is a new player in this increasingly corporatized game, rising up in the spaces created between a deteriorating environment and a "structurally adjusted" adult education that serves the needs of the global market. It is a hybrid outgrowth of the environmental movement and adult education, combining an ecological orientation with a learning paradigm to provide a vigorous educational approach to environmental concerns. Far from being neutral, environmental adult education requires that "commitment and action must be the ultimate aim of any educative practice" (Finger, 1989, p. 27). The commitment and action of environmental adult education finds a natural home in the struggle for community sustainability.

Meeting the Challenges: A New Framework for Sustainability

The global challenges posed to community sustainability and environmental adult education seem overwhelming. As powerful transnational interests shape the future of both communities and the environment, a new framework for sustainability that incorporates the commitment and action of environmental adult education must be developed to meet these challenges.

Sustainability. Although flabby with overuse, *sustainability* is a term that still resonates deeply with many people. It projects the hopes and fears that humans carry about their present life and about the future world of their children and grandchildren. Although seen by different people in different ways, sustainability involves "*a set of structures and processes that build the civil commons. The civil commons is society's organized and community-funded capacity of universally accessible resources to provide for the life preservation and growth of society's members and their environmental life-host.* The civil commons is, in other words, what people ensure together as a society to protect and further life, as distinct from money aggregates" (McMurtry, 1998, p. 24).

Public education, the Kyoto Agreement, nature preserves, environmental laws, the Endangered Species Act, and clean water regulations are just some examples of the "conscious and co-operative human agency" (McMurtry, 1999a, p. 205) of the civil commons. Such conscious human agency can work to prevent the destruction of not only human communities but also the environment—the basis of all life on earth and the ultimate ground of any notion of sustainability. This agency ranges from "environmental activism on the ground to international protocols to protect the ozone layer and emerging initiatives for environmental standards in international trade treaties" (McMurtry, 1999a, p. 214).

In this age of corporate globalization, however, economic policies such as comparative advantage completely separate consumers from the origins of the products they buy. On many levels, the environment has become an externality, not only for transnational corporations but also for individuals and communities. We have become distanced and alienated from the very basis of life. One example of such an alienated view of the world, reported by Lee (1993), is that "trees may grow faster in bank accounts than they do in the woods" (p. 562). In other words: "Harvesting populations at unsustainable speed, mining the resource, can be rational if the earnings from harvest produce financial assets whose value appreciates more rapidly than the resource would regenerate" (p. 562).

An antidote to this alienation, the civil commons embraces what McMurtry (1998) calls life values—that is, values that promote life first and foremost. Choosing for life values can counter the monetary values that drive corporate globalization, exposing their limitations, especially with respect to their inability to recognize the importance of human and environmental life, except insofar as they can be used to maximize corporate profits.

As a way of engaging with the world that promotes a life-affirming interconnectedness, the civil commons encompasses the idea that if the environment is threatened, so is human life. But in a telling reversal from the human situation, it is not what we *do* to the environment, but what we *don't do*.

"The way in which humans can sustain their environmental life-host, then, is not by providing for *its* means of life, for this is not required or possible. The only way in which *sustainability* of the environmental life-sequence can be achieved is by humans *not systemically depleting, polluting, or destroying* it" (McMurtry, 1999a, p. 160).

Sustainability would not even be an issue without human destruction of the environment, especially the kind of destruction carried out in the name of economic "efficiency" demanded by corporate globalization. The global market system can be seen to be carcinogenic in its pattern to the extent that it strips, as it does now, the evolving civil commons of its effective means of environmental protection (McMurtry, 1999a, p. 216).

If we understand sustainability as involving a set of structures and processes that build the civil commons, we can immediately see that working to preserve and enhance the "co-operative human construction that protects and/or enables universal access to life goods" (McMurtry, 1999b, p. 1) is the key to environmental protection and human well-being. While policies based on the money values of corporate globalization can wreak havoc on the environment, policies based on the life values of the civil commons can protect it. Indeed, according to McMurtry (1998, p. 380), the civil commons is "the sole protector of society's environmental life-host," so any attack on the civil commons is an attack on global life itself. Around the world, people are working together to stave off such attacks by contributing to the civil commons through the process of learning their way into sustainability.

Environmental Learning and Sustainability. Orr (1992, pp. x–xi) argues that while schooling is what happens in school and colleges, and training represents the inculcation of rote habit, learning "is what can happen throughout life for those willing to risk it." In the age of corporate globalization, however, the ecological dimension is often missing from learning initiatives, which tend to concentrate on "learning for earning." The missing ecological dimension would help us to understand that, above all, we are "unavoidably organically embodied and ecologically 'embedded'" (Benton, 1994, p. 41). Lack of understanding of this environmental imperative has contributed to the ecological crisis we are currently experiencing, which Orr (1992, p. x) would argue represents, in large measure, a failure of education. This pedagogical failure can be overcome by an environmental adult education oriented to commitment and action that incorporates a form of environmental learning devoted to the same aims. Such learning would consider the commitment as lifelong and the action as worth the risk because it includes the missing ecological dimension.

While learning is crucial to achieving sustainability, often it is neither recognized as important nor seen to be even happening. When examining the interactive processes in a rural community, Falk and Kilpatrick (2000) "were struck by the fact that a great deal of learning was occurring, yet it went largely unrecognized" (p. 97). Such lack of recognition must be overcome if we are to place learning at the heart of sustainability. Following Serrano (2000), we need to understand that "every social encounter anywhere, at any level or arena, is an opportunity for learning" (pp. 93–94). Learning must become a way of life if we are to learn our way into sustainability.

Such learning, however, must break free from the dominant corporate ethic that is spreading like a cancer around the world (McMurtry, 1999a).

But breaking free will be difficult for those raised within this ethic. Mische (1992) warns: "It is no trivial matter to change the underlying structures of thought in which we have been schooled, and which at deep and often unconscious levels affect our fundamental patterns of seeing and being on the planet. The change amounts to a revolution in human learning" (p. 10).

Environmental learning can enable a revolution in learning if it is reconceptualized within an understanding of sustainability as a set of structures and processes that build the civil commons. Like sustainability itself, environmental learning would be grounded by the anchors of critical reflection, dialogue, and life values. Critical reflection would remove its neutral veneer by questioning dominant ways of seeing and being in the world. Dialogue would open up the opportunity for both educators and learners to participate together in building community sustainability. Life values would provide an orientation toward preserving life, not increasing money, as the new way of seeing and being in the world. Together, these three anchors would infuse environmental learning with a critical, participatory, life-affirming vigor that centers on the environment and builds sustainability. In this way, environmental learning could live up to the aims of commitment and action that characterize the practice of environmental adult education.

Such a reconceptualization moves environmental learning from an individual orientation and allies it with the kind of critical social learning advocated by Serrano (2000). It also connects environmental learning to transformative learning by promoting new ways of seeing and being in the world. In this way, environmental learning becomes a kind of sustainable learning, one of the processes that contributes to the civil commons, which can counter the narrowed learning perspectives that promote, and are promoted by, corporate globalization.

Environmental Adult Education: Grounded in the Local and Embracing the Global

As the economy goes global, opposition to its corrosive impacts spreads around the world. While this opposition emerges from diverse local interests, it often centers on environmental concerns—clean water, breathable air, intact rainforests, uncontaminated foods. These concerns form a rallying point for critical analysis, global networking, and learning our way into new ways of seeing and being—not just in local communities but on the whole planet.

Orr (1992) argues that "education appropriate for sustainability will give greater emphasis to place-specific knowledge and skills useful in meeting individual local needs, and for rebuilding local communities" (p. 146). This is where environmental adult education can ground itself: within local communities. From that firm grounding, environmental adult education can reach out and embrace other localities, eventually joining in a global environmental pedagogy. Such a pedagogy, based in the commitment and action of environmental adult education, can contribute to community sustainability and oppose the "enclosure" of the civil commons by the policies of corporate globalization.

References

Allen, P. L., and Sachs, C. E. "The Social Side of Sustainability: Class, Gender and Race." *Science as Culture,* 1991, *2,* 569–590.

Benton, T. "Biology and Social Theory in the Environmental Debate." In T. Benton and M. Redclift (eds.), *Social Theory and the Global Environment.* New York: Routledge, 1994.

Brecher, J., Costello, T., and Smith, B. *Globalization from Below: The Power of Solidarity.* Boston: South End Press, 2000.

Daly, H. E. "Globalization Versus Internationalization—Some Implications." *Ecological Economics,* 1999, *31,* 31–37.

Ellwood, W. *The No-Nonsense Guide to Globalization.* Toronto: New Internationalist Publications and Between the Lines, 2001.

Falk, I., and Kilpatrick, S. "What *Is* Social Capital? A Study of Interaction in a Rural Community." *Sociologia Ruralis,* 2000, *40*(1), 87–110.

Finger, M. "Environmental Adult Education from the Perspective of the Adult Learner." *Convergence,* 1989, *22*(4), 25–31.

Foley, G. "Radical Adult Education and Learning." *International Journal of Lifelong Education,* 2001, *20*(1/2), 71–88.

"Globalism Project." Parkland Institute, University of Alberta, Canada. [http://www.ualberta.ca/~parkland/mcri.html]. 2001.

Goldsmith, E. "Can the Environment Survive the Global Economy?" *The Ecologist,* 1997, *27*(6), 242–248.

Lee, K. N. "Greed, Scale Mismatch, and Learning." *Ecological Applications,* 1993, *3*(4), 560–564.

McMurtry, J. *Unequal Freedoms: The Global Market as an Ethical System.* Toronto: Garamond Press, 1998.

McMurtry, J. *The Cancer Stage of Capitalism.* London: Pluto Press, 1999a.

McMurtry, J. "The Lifeground, the Civil Commons, and Global Development." Paper presented at the annual meeting of the Canadian Association for Studies in International Development, Congress of the Social Sciences and Humanities, Sherbrooke, Quebec, June 7, 1999b.

Mische, P. M. "Toward a Pedagogy of Ecological Responsibility: Learning to Reinhabit the Earth." *Convergence,* 1992, *25*(2), 9–23.

Orr, D. W. *Ecological Literacy: Education and the Transition to a Postmodern World.* Albany: State University of New York Press, 1992.

Redclift, M. "Sustainability and Sociology: Northern Preoccupations." In E. Becker and T. Jahn (eds.), *Sustainability and the Social Sciences: A Cross-Disciplinary Approach to Integrating Environmental Considerations into Theoretical Reorientation.* New York: Zed Books, 1999.

Serrano, I. "Learning Sustainability from Crisis." *Convergence,* 2000, *33*(1–2), 78–101.

Shaker, E. "The Privatization of Post-Secondary Institutions." *Education, Limited,* 1999, *1*(4), ii–ix.

Sumner, J. "Community Sustainability and Adult Education: Learning to Build Civil Capital and Resist Corporate Globalization." *Australian Journal of Adult and Community Education,* 2000, *40*(2), 53–65.

JENNIFER SUMNER *teaches in the School of Rural Extension Studies at the University of Guelph, Ontario, Canada.*

5

Practical and theoretical considerations of activist-educators using environmental popular education in indigenous social movements in India are explored. The responses of these social movements to destructive development are linked with the theoretical dialogue on environmental adult education and social transformation.

Environmental Popular Education and Indigenous Social Movements in India

Dip Kapoor

This chapter examines the theoretical and practical links between environmental education, popular education, and the development of indigenous social movements in the Indian context, with specific reference to the Kondh Adivasis, indigenous people and original dwellers of the state of Orissa. Practical and theoretical implications regarding the use of environmental popular education (EPE) in social movements that engage in constructive resistance to state and corporate-led development and modernization are considered with the view to inform practice and the theoretical discussion regarding environmental adult education, social movements, and social transformation.

Popular education is defined in terms of its recognition of the relations between knowledge and power, structure and agency, and recognition that adult education can play a part in challenging oppressive social relations such as those that characterize the Adivasi experience in India (Schugurensky, 2000; Mayo, 1999). It is based on the premise that the act of teaching and learning is political and that the purpose of a participatory, dialogical problem-posing education that is grounded in people's experience, knowledge, and daily lived experience, is to democratize and reconfigure concentrations of power that are oppressive and dehumanizing (Barndt, 1995; Clover, 1995; Clover, Follen, and Hall, 2000; Hall and Sullivan, 1994). Ideally, through this process Adivasis begin to question underlying hegemonic assumptions used to justify oppression, and this creates the possibility of praxis in the form of collective responses aimed at transforming oppressive power and asserting local aspirations (Barndt, 1991; Freire, 1977).

NEW DIRECTIONS FOR ADULT AND CONTINUING EDUCATION, no. 99, Fall 2003 © Wiley Periodicals, Inc.

After developing a brief contextual description of postindependence development and the social movement responses to "destructive development" by Adivasis in India, specific illustrations pertaining to the use of EPE in the Kondh movement will be developed, with an emphasis on the importance and place of Kondh cosmological and ecological knowledge within the educational process. It is suggested that EPE, through a process of democratic dialogue, can help to inspire localized Adivasi movements to become part of a wider encounter with the hegemonic aspirations of a developmentalist state, in the interests of freeing cultural, material, and ecological space for the Adivasi.

Postindependence Development in India and Adivasi Social Movement Responses

When India achieved independence from the British in 1947, Jawaharlal Nehru, its first prime minister, proclaimed to the nation that India had kept her tryst with destiny. From its inception, the Indian state was confronted by two different visions for reconstruction, (1) the Gandhian project of reviving the village economy as the basis for development, and (2) the Nehruvian plan for prosperity through rapid industrialization. The ruling Congress party adopted the "industrialize or perish" model of economic development in its second five-year plan. From the second plan onwards, the Indian government spent only 22 percent of its total budget on agriculture, even though 75 percent of the population was engaged in agriculture. The greater share of the plan's budget outlay was consistently invested to develop industries, which employed a mere 11 percent of the population (Kohli, 1987). Indian nationalists believed that India's reconstruction could come about only through an emulation of the West, intellectually through the infusion of modern science, and materially through the adoption of large-scale industrialization (Gadgil and Guha, 1992).

In the name of national development, India's Adivasis have had to pay the price for this choice made by others that involved little or no regard for their aspirations. With a population of 58 million representing 8 percent of the total population of India, the Indian constitution (under Article 342) recognizes 427 scheduled tribes (Adivasis) and promises to protect them from social injustice and exploitation (Article 46), while providing a financial guarantee for tribal development schemes (Article 273) (Tripathi, 1999; Rizvi and Roy, 1998). However, despite Jawaharlal Nehru's assurances that tribal rights to land and forests would be respected and that they should be allowed to develop along the lines of their own genius with no government imposition, the tenor of successive five-year plans has been to hasten tribal assimilation (Chakravarty, 1996; Tripathi, 1999).

Gadgil and Guha (1992) note that Adivasi traditional rights to land and forests for subsistence provision have been addressed through a complex scheme of land reclassification that has essentially led to the detribalization of tribal forestland, as Adivasi rights to the forest were reduced to grudging concessions granted by the state or an outright denial of tenure or access. They conclude that the removal of forests from the traditional Adivasi moral economy of subsistence provision and their assimilation into the modern state-industry political economy for profit, has undermined the conditions conducive to sustainable use of land and forests.

Some 90 percent of all mining operations are located in the interior forest and predominantly Adivasi regions of India. Forests have also been flooded in dam-development schemes. India engaged in 246 major and 1,059 medium irrigation projects between 1947 and 1982 and is known as the largest dam builder in the world (Fernandes and Thukral, 1989). The notorious Narmada River Valley Project will entail the submergence of 350,000 hectares of forests and 200,000 hectares of agricultural and other land, and displace some two million people (Baviskar, 1995; Kothari and Parajuli, 1993). India has been losing 1.5 million hectares of forest cover every year, and the rate of deforestation is increasing yearly (Chowdhary, 1989). Forest cover was reduced to 22 percent of land area in 1952 from 40 percent in 1854. In the late 1980s, aerial surveys demonstrated that only 8 to 10 percent of India's land was covered with closed forests (Omvedt, 1987). While 4 million hectares were "lost" between 1951 and 1976, some 23 million more were cut down between 1976 and 1992 (Gadgil and Guha, 1992; United Nations Development Programme, 1992). This accelerating rate of deforestation means that Adivasis have been forced out of the forests and into settled cultivation, and these people primarily belong to the 60 percent of Indians who are poor peasants or landless laborers (Omvedt, 1982).

The development process in India has increasingly pitted the uncertain fruits of modernization, industrialization, dam construction, and deforestation against the integrity of community, culture, and ecology. Kothari (1986) and Nandy (1984) argue that state-led postindependence development has led to a massive erosion of the ecological basis of Indian civilization. The process of economic development has led to the pauperization, dislocation, even destruction of many subordinate groups and traditional communities in India and the forests that have sustained their way of life (Routledge, 1987). According to one conservative estimate, the total number of people, including Adivasis, displaced for development projects since independence is 15.5 million, 75 percent of whom have yet to be rehabilitated (Fernandes and Thukral, 1989).

The conflict that ensued from this process has led to the emergence of numerous social movements throughout India (Dhanagre, 1983; Oommen, 1990; Rao, 1979; Shah, 1990), including Adivasi movements (Duyker, 1987; Singh, 1982, 1983, 1985; International Work Group for Indigenous Affairs, 1986). They are a response, in part, to the political, social, economic, cultural, and ecological processes set in motion by the development juggernaut of the Indian state. At times they are also a response to the incapacity or refusal of the state to provide adequate solutions to the dilemmas experienced by affected communities. Social movements represent struggles for cultural, ecological, and economic survival, as indigenous people are confronted by the apparatus of exploitation, domination, and repression in a seemingly inexorable process beyond their control (Routledge, 1993).

These place-specific social movements are often involved in constructive resistance (Parajuli, 1990; Routledge, 1993). Not only do they articulate dissent, and often noncompliance, with central and state government policies, but they also actively seek to articulate and implement alternative development practices. Viewing state-directed development processes as inimical to local tradition and livelihood, many of these movements actively affirm local identity, culture, and systems of knowledge as an integral part of their resistance. For instance, the Adivasi movements in the Jharkhand region working against dam construction and deforestation have advocated for use of agriculture and water management systems based on more prudent indigenous irrigation schemes and ecological practices (Parajuli, 1990, 1991).

Similar Adivasi and ecological movements include the Appiko movement against illegal overfelling of forests in the state of Karnataka (Hegde, 1989), the Chipko peasant movement in Uttarkhand that emerged in the early 1970s in response to deforestation and the impact on local economy and culture (Berreman, 1985; Routledge, 1993), antidrought and desertification movements in the provinces of Rajasthan, Orissa, Karnataka, and Maharashtra (Bandyopadhyay and Shiva, 1988), the movement by the Bhilala Adivasis against the Narmada River Valley Dam Project in Gujarat and Madhya Pradesh (Baviskar, 1995), and several Adivasi dam-related movements protesting against the Tehri, Bodhghat, Koel Karo, Inchampalli, and Bhopalpatnam dams in other states (Asia Watch, 1992). Other examples include the Gandhamadan Adivasi movement against Bharat Aluminum Company (BALCO) in Orissa and the struggle against deforestation and displacement (Desai, 1991), and several other pre- and postindependence Adivasi struggles centered around forest ecology, political autonomy, and cultural identity (D'Monte, 1989; Singh, 1982, 1983).

Theoretical and Practical Considerations for EPE and Indigenous Social Movements

The synergy between environmental and natural concerns around (1) deforestation and land cultivation and (2) popular and social questions of disempowerment, silence, cultural identity, and loss of the means to reproduce a material existence has made it possible for EPE to find a place in Adivasi social movement responses to destructive development. The following discussion on the theoretical and practical considerations pertaining to the use of EPE in Adivasi social movements is informed by the literature on environmental popular education and social movements in India and by the author's continued association with a Kondh Adivasi social movement in the coastal state of Orissa, India. This movement has consciously employed a process of EPE over the past five years with the help of a group of ten Adivasi activist-educators (Kapoor, 2000).

A Prefigurative Role for EPE in Adivasi Social Movement Formation

Nandy (1989) notes that the development of the state is equated with the development process in general. Consequently, the Indian state takes possession of and consumes an increasing proportion of these resources. This hegemonic development process has an inherently spatial character in that it involves appropriation, domination, and production processes in the interests of gaining control of property and financial capital by the state's ruling elites (Harvey, 1990). The resulting conflict has given rise to social movements that aim to liberate cultural, material, and ecological space by resisting the oppressive processes of domination.

The attempt by a hegemonic bloc composed of elites to control cultural, material, and ecological space and capital has given rise to social movement challenges to break the limits of such a system of oppressive social relations (Cox, 1987; Melucci, 1989). In this sense, social movements may be viewed as agents of counterhegemony because they expose hegemonic methods that work in various ways to coerce the oppressed to accept or "consent" to their own exploitation and daily misery (Boggs, 1976). Counterhegemonic challenges and transgressions in the form of social movements entail a disorganization of such consent; a disruption of the hegemonic discourse and practices of capital (Carroll, 1997).

As a primarily hunter-gatherer society that has very recently taken to settled agriculture, the Kondhs have always and still rely on the forests. According to sketchy historical and anthropological records, they have been steadily retreating ever farther into the forested hills of the Eastern Ghats since 4000 B.C. to escape from Dravidian and then Aryan invaders and finally the British and the postindependence developmentalist Indian state (Nayak, Boal, and Soreng, 1990). The Kondhs engaged in the specific partnership discussed here have faced multiple displacements imposed to make room over the past decade for corporate bamboo plantations and for the development of a wildlife reserve to promote tourism in the area. As forests have disappeared and fewer places are left for refuge, a sense has developed among these Adivasis that the time has come to stand their ground. EPE draws its initial impetus from this general assessment of their situation by the Kondhs and plays an important prefigurative role in helping to create a conscious sense of the possibility for collective, coordinated, and directed action in the form of organized resistance to defend, if not roll back, hegemonic control of biophysical and cultural space by a developmentalist state (Gramsci, 1971; Mayo, 1999).

Kondh Cosmological Knowledge and Critical Social-Structural Reflection

Kondh cosmological explanations and belief regarding their current ecological and cultural plight and social-structural explanations for environmental degradation and Kondh marginalization both help define the critical dialogue between Kondhs and activist-educators, a dialogue that prompts associated courses of action to bring about social-structural and environmental change. Dichotomous themes pertaining to deforestation and aforestation; traditional shifting cultivation, named *podu,* and landlessness; and hunting and gathering are embedded in traditional songs employed by the activist-educators and in ritual symbols—such as the *meriah post* used for animal sacrifices to the earth deity and the Darni stones symbolic of *Darni,* the earth deity—which are located in each village. These traditional symbols are used in conjunction with each other to stimulate dialogue, problem identification, and discussion of contradictions in the lived experience of the Adivasis as it pertains to their deteriorating relationship with the forest, the land, and the Gods and ancestors who are their protectors and diviners of their well-being or destruction.

In unpacking traditional symbols like the *Kui* songs in the Kondh language, the *meriah post,* and the Darni stones, the activist-educators and Kondhs engage in dialogue that emphasizes the spiritual beliefs of the Kondhs to explain why the forests are disappearing and question why availability of land and *podu* cultivation are becoming problematic. Kondhs recount and reflect on their beliefs and spiritual connection to the land and the forests. Dialogue centers on Kondh mythology, which suggests that Darni emerged from the earth as the first Kondh woman and then at her own request became the first human meriah, or sacrifice, in order to ensure fertility of the forests and land for the Kondh people. She holds the dual role of deity and symbolic founder of the Kondh people. Lineal descent from Darni and from the land gives Kondhs the conviction that the forest and land are the natural source of all life/their life and their reason for living. The gods, the spirits of ancestors, all living creatures, the natural environment, and the past and present are united in a sacred trust for the Kondhs, a trust that is justified by the central significance of Darni, the earth deity and creator.

Deforestation, landlessness and dispossession, and crop failure are explained in terms of failing to be worthy of Darni's protection and the displeasure of ancestors because the Kondhs have failed to maintain the right balance between their lives and their spiritual commitment to the natural world. Action to alleviate this situation demands renewing these connections through ritual and sacrifice and through greater efforts to seek the grace and protection of the ancestors. For instance, Kondhs often express a sense of guilt about their shift from a hunter-gatherer subsistence economy to one of settled cultivation, or *podu.* The priest reminds participants of the significance of the *meriah* sacrifice to the earth deity by repeating the opening lines of the ritual: "We cultivated your earth, we defiled you, so take this buffalo and eat it. Make our corn grow, don't bring sickness and trouble."

The principle behind EPE remains the valorization of such local knowledge and power as the basis for sustainable communities. While such approaches begin at the local level, they also incorporate analysis of power inequalities driving environmental degradation. As Barndt (1995) states: "Environmental education offers this tension to popular education, which has been charged (often justifiably) as being anthropocentric. A popular environmental education challenges the power relations underlying the dominant system of development and seeks to reframe and reestablish the nature-culture connection in the way we think and act with each other and the planet" (p. 26).

Cosmological reflection is combined with critical social-structural reflection as activist-educators utilize contemporary symbols to encourage Kondhs to share stories about their encounters with representatives of state agencies such as the Forest Department or Revenue Department. This line of inquiry is used to provide a brief historical view of dispossession and the role of the state and law in this regard. State forest policies become a part of the dialogue as activist-educators explain that village forests have been established to provide tribal peoples with timber for firewood, land for grazing cattle, and other local needs but that this land classification is being eroded by the encroachment of other classifications. For example, reserved forests are being reclassified to meet the demands of national defense, communications, industry, and other purposes of public importance. Tribal peoples no longer have legal rights in these forests, and the amount of forestland being placed under this new classification is increasing due to the expansionist development policy of the state (Kapoor, 2000).

Popular education makes the struggle against hegemony by subordinate groups engaged in social movement action possible by helping them to penetrate the false and irrational world of social appearances tied to the dominant order and by helping to create a new universe of belief systems, cultural values, and social relations (Boggs, 1984; Mayo, 1999). Popular education aims at unveiling objective reality, which creates the basis for a new apprehension of the world and a disposition to change it, but such revelation is authentic only when it constitutes a dynamic and dialectical unity with the practice of transforming reality (Freire, 1994, 1970). That is, Kondhs' collective action to change this revealed objective reality has resulted in their being able to increase their control over land and forests for the communities that are part of this movement and develop an evolving sense of social-psychological confidence (Kapoor, 2000).

Kondh Ecological Knowledge and Practice

EPE also promotes a dialogue between systematized, "objective" scientific knowledge and popular knowledge in an effort to conscientize people submerged in a culture of silence to emerge as conscious makers of their own history and culture (Schugurensky, 2000; Mayo, 1999). The role of Kondh cosmological knowledge has been described here, and EPE builds on these understandings to reify Kondh ecological practices.

In many instances, activist-educators learn about agricultural and forestry practices from the experiential-empirical knowledge of the Kondhs, while weaving in scientific understanding when and where it is appropriate from the standpoint of the Kondhs. Activist-educators are conscious of Western, or Euro-American, dominance of what constitutes valid knowledge and how such knowledge is produced and disseminated, and they are also cognizant of the concomitant deprivileging and negation of local and indigenous knowledges (Dei, 1995). They are prepared to assist local peoples on their own terms.

Soil fertility is enhanced in Kondh agricultural practices in several ways. For example, nitrogen is replenished in the soil through crop rotation by following rice paddy cultivation with the growing of lentils, in recognition of symbiotic relationships between ragi millet and lentils that develop when they are grown together. Mixed cropping and graded harvesting with as many as twelve crops are also practiced, and the land is nourished by leaf compost and manure from cow, goat, and chicken dung. Mustard seeds, which are known to leach the soil of nutrients, are never grown on the same patch repeatedly.

While Kondhs develop diagonal plots on the hills and slopes to prevent rapid water runoff and soil erosion, they also practice shifting cultivation on small plots and are not convinced about the negative impact of this practice. Activist-educators point out related problems such as deforestation, soil erosion, and water runoff. Overutilization of small plots is also problematic because there is little chance of revitalizing the soil. The traditional practice of ten- to twelve-year cycles before reuse is no longer possible due to constraints on land availability. However, Kondhs have now assessed and determined the utility of growing vena, a grass with a long root system that was introduced by the activist-educators as a means to prevent soil erosion and increase the water-holding capacity of land in the hillside shifting-cultivation area.

Aforestation measures in the form of fruit orchards and planting of fast-growing fuel-wood trees and respecting trees with cosmological and productive significance—such as mango, sal, and mahul trees—have been embraced by the Adivasi communities. When women collect firewood, they restrict themselves to dead branches and do not cut living wood from trees. Certain forested areas of spiritual and ancestral significance are always left untouched no matter the circumstance. Trees are noted and named, and the community carefully harvests forest products by taking turns with specific trees and zones as determined by the season, the age of trees, and community needs. People are conscious of the need to allow for forest regeneration, no matter how pressing their current needs may be, and often endure considerable hardship by doing without during times of environmental distress such as when cyclones deforest the area.

EPE recognizes people's knowledge and agricultural practices and actively incorporates them as an integral part of the educational exchange that takes place between Kondhs and the activist-educators. While the latter bring scientific-systematic knowledge to the dialogue concerning, for example, the ecological impact of shifting cultivation, Kondhs make the final decisions regarding their forestry and agricultural practices after engaging in careful deliberation.

EPE and Indigenous Social Movements

EPE helps to initiate, define, develop, and glue together Adivasi social movements, thereby improving the prospects for environmental and social change. As a continual process of reflection and action between environmental popular educators and an Adivasi community, EPE builds the scaffolding for the movement by initiating a conscious, critically reflective, and organized opportunity to channel and transform spontaneous eruptions of defiance and frustration with ecological and sociopolitical domination into real prospects for socioenvironmental change. The knowledge of the Adivasi is central to this exchange, both from an ecological, and a sociopolitical and cultural standpoint, as is the scientific and social perspective brought to the engagement by the activist-educator.

By connecting concerns about ecological degradation, subsistence, and sociocultural marginalization, a process of EPE has the potential to inspire "localized" Adivasi movements to appreciate the importance of taking part in a wider struggle against the hegemony of the state and corporate-led development, which are marginalizing the tribal and destroying the forests and their cultural autonomy. The transformatory potential of social movements like that of the Kondhs, however, lies in their collective ability to affect multiple, infinitesimal changes in power structures, thereby helping to construct a new power base (Sklair, 1995). In terms of a politics of radical democracy, such movements need to find ways of globalizing these disruptions by forming a historic bloc of social movement in order to expand the impact of localized resistances with the view to protect the environment and the Adivasi. EPE can help to build this counterhegemonic challenge to global capital and state-led destructive development, in order to free cultural, material, and ecological space for Adivasis, thereby improving environmental prospects by returning the forests to those who leave the smallest ecological footprint (Sachs, 1997).

References

Asia Watch. *Before the Deluge: Human Rights Abuses at India's Naramada Dam*. New York: Human Rights Watch, 1992.

Bandyopadhyay, J., and Shiva, V. "Political Economy of Ecology Movements." *Economic and Political Weekly,* 1988, *23,* 1223–1232.

Barndt, D. *To Change This House: Popular Education Under the Sandinistas.* Toronto: Between the Lines, 1991.

Barndt, D. "Critical Education for Social Change in the Context of Sustainable Development." In N. Singh and V. Titi (eds.), *Empowerment Towards Sustainable Development.* Winnipeg, Canada: Winnipeg International Institute for Sustainable Development, 1995.

Baviskar, A. *In the Belly of the River: Tribal Conflicts Over Development in the Narmada Valley.* Oxford: Oxford University Press, 1995.

Berreman, G. "Chipko: Nonviolent Direct Action to Save the Himalayas." *South Asia Bulletin,* 1985, *5*(2), 8–13.

Boggs, C. *Gramsci's Marxism.* London: Pluto, 1976.

Boggs, C. *The Two Revolutions: Gramsci and the Dilemmas of Western Marxism.* Boston: South End Press, 1984.

Carroll, W. (ed.). *Organizing Dissent: Contemporary Social Movement in Theory and in Practice.* Toronto: Garamond Press, 1997.

Chakravarty, K. (ed.). *Tribal Identity in India: Extinction or Adaptation.* Bhopal, India: Indira Gandhi Rashtriya Manav Sangrahalaya, 1996.

Chowdhary, K. "Poverty, Environment and Development." *Daedalus,* 1989, *118*(1), 141–158.

Clover, D. E. "Theoretical Foundations and Practice of Critical Environmental Adult Education in Canada." *Convergence,* 1995, *28*(4), 44–54.

Clover, D. E., Follen, S., and Hall, B. *The Nature of Transformation: Environmental Adult Education.* (2nd ed.) Toronto: University of Toronto Press, 2000.

Cox, R. *Production, Power, and the World Order.* New York: Columbia University Press, 1987.

Dei, G. "Indigenous Knowledge as an Empowerment Tool for Sustainable Development." In V. Titi and N. Singh (eds.), *Empowerment for Sustainable Development: Towards Operational Strategies.* Halifax, Canada: Fernwood Publishing, 1995.

Desai, N. "Nonviolent People's Struggles in India." In B. Martin, S. Anderson, and J. Larmore (eds.), *Nonviolent Struggle and Social Defence.* London: War Resisters International, 1991.

Dhanagre, D. N. *Peasant Movements in India 1920–1950.* Oxford: Oxford University Press, 1983.

D'Monte, D. "Green at the Roots." *Seminar,* 1989, *355,* 16–20.

Duyker, E. *Tribal Guerrillas.* Oxford: Oxford University Press, 1987.

Fernandes, W., and Thukral, E. (eds.). *Development, Displacement and Rehabilitation.* New Delhi, India: Indian Social Institute, 1989.

Freire, P. *Pedagogy of the Oppressed.* New York: Continuum, 1970.

Freire, P. *Cultural Action for Freedom.* Harmondsworth, England: Penguin Books, 1977.

Freire, P. *Pedagogy of Hope: Revisiting Pedagogy of the Oppressed.* New York: Continuum, 1994.

Gadgil, M., and Guha, R. *This Fissured Land: An Ecological History of India.* Oxford: Oxford University Press, 1992.

Gramsci, A. *Selections from the Prison Notebooks of Antonio Gramsci.* (Q. Hoare and G. Nowell Smith, ed. and trans.) New York: International Publishers, 1971.

Hall, B., and O'Sullivan, E.V. "Transformative Learning: Contexts and Practices." In *Awakening Sleepy Knowledge.* Toronto: Transformative Learning Centre, Ontario Institute for Studies in Education, 1994.

Harvey, D. *The Condition of Postmodernity.* Oxford, England: Blackwell, 1990.

Hegde, P. "The Appiko Movement: Forest Conservation in Southern India." *Cultural Survival Quarterly,* 1989, *13*(2), 29–30.

International Work Group for Indigenous Affairs (IWGIA). *The Naga Nation and Its*

Struggle Against Genocide. IWGIA Document, no. 56. Copenhagen: International Work Group for Indigenous Affairs, 1986.

Kapoor, D. "Environmental Popular Education and Indigenous Activism in India." *Convergence,* 2000, *33*(3), 32–43.

Kohli, A. *The State and Poverty in India: The Politics of Reform.* Cambridge, England: Cambridge University Press, 1987.

Kothari, R. "Masses, Classes, and the State." *Economic and Political Weekly,* 1986, *21,* 210–216.

Kothari, S., and Parajuli, P. "No Nature Without Social Justice: A Plea for Cultural and Ecological Pluralism in India." In W. Sachs (ed.), *Global Ecology. A New Arena of Political Conflict.* London: Zed Books, 1993.

Mayo, P. *Gramsci, Freire, and Adult Education: Possibilities for Transformative Action.* London: Zed Books, 1999.

Melucci, A. *Nomads of the Present: Social Movements and Individual Needs in Contemporary Society.* Philadelphia: Temple University Press, 1989.

Nandy, A. "Culture, State, and Rediscovery of Indian Politics." *Economic and Political Weekly,* 1984, *19*(49), 2078–2083.

Nandy, A. "The Political Culture of the Indian State." *Daedalus,* 1989, *118*(4), 1–26.

Nayak, R., Boal, B., and Soreng, N. *The Kondhs: A Handbook for Development.* New Delhi, India: Indian Social Institute, 1990.

Omvedt, G. *Land, Caste and Politics in Indian States.* New Delhi, India: Authors Guild Press, 1982.

Omvedt, G. "India's Green Movements." *Race and Class,* 1987, *28*(4), 29–38.

Oommen, T. K. *Protest and Change: Studies in Social Movements.* New Delhi, India: Sage, 1990.

Parajuli, P. "Grassroots Movements and Popular Education in Jharkhand, India." Unpublished doctoral dissertation, Stanford University, 1990.

Parajuli, P. "Power and Knowledge in Development Discourse: New Social Movements and the State in India." *International Conflict Research,* 1991, *127,* 173–190.

Rao, M.S.A. (ed.). *Social Movements in India.* New Delhi, India: Manohar Press, 1979.

Rizvi, S., and Roy, S. *India: Scheduled Tribes.* New Delhi, India: B. R. Publishing, 1998.

Routledge, P. "Modernity as a Vision of Conquest: Development and Culture in India." *Cultural Survival Quarterly,* 1987, *11*(3), 63–66.

Routledge, P. *Terrains of Resistance: Nonviolent Social Movements and the Contestation of Place in India.* London: Praeger, 1993.

Sachs, W. "The Need for the Home Perspective." In M. Rahnema and V. Bawtree (eds.), *The Post-Development Reader.* London: Zed Books, 1997.

Schugurensky, D. "Adult Education and Social Transformation: On Gramsci, Freire, and the Challenge of Comparing Comparisons." *Comparative Education Review,* 2000, *44*(4), 515–522.

Shah, G. *Social Movements in India: A Review of the Literature.* New Delhi, India: Sage, 1990.

Singh, K. S. *Tribal Movements in India.* Vol. 1. New Delhi, India: Manohar Press, 1982.

Singh, K. S. *Tribal Movements in India.* Vol. 2. New Delhi, India: Manohar Press, 1983.

Singh, K. S. *Tribal Society in India: An Anthropo-Historical Perspective.* New Delhi, India: Manohar Press, 1985.

Sklair, L. "Social Movements and Global Capitalism." *Sociology,* 1995, *29*(3), 495–512.

Tripathi, R. *A History of Ancient India.* Delhi, India: Motilal Banarsidass, 1999.

United Nations Development Programme. *Human Development Report 1992.* New York: Oxford University Press, 1992.

DIP KAPOOR *is an adjunct associate professor in educational policy studies at the University of Alberta and president of HELP, a voluntary development organization currently working in partnership with Adivasis in India.*

6

When women who share common concerns for the environment come together, powerful learning occurs through critical reflection on tensions between daily-life decisions and emotional connections to social and ecological concerns.

Environmental Adult Education: Women Living the Tensions

Lee Karlovic, Kathryn Patrick

Seven women adult educators with a common concern for the environment were brought together to examine their own abilities to balance ethical and pragmatic tensions between their "everyday lives" and the urgent need to take action to protect the environment. What happens when women trained in and/or working in adult and popular education focus as a group on the environment through an examination of the connections among women, the environment, and education? The authors' assumption was that participation in this project could increase environmental awareness and inform other educators who want to attract women concerned about the environment to become environmental adult educators.

Background

In the twenty-first century, it has become increasingly difficult to keep ourselves informed about public policy decisions that are marketed to the public like so many consumer products. While many North Americans may have as many as 150 television channels to watch, the news they hear is recycled on the half hour. Newspapers are generally owned by only a handful of wealthy conglomerates that garner their news from one or two sources such as the Associated Press. The tension between owning the newest in technology, as embodied in large, gas-guzzling vehicles, and sending a donation to Greenpeace is one that North Americans live with each day. We experience the benefits of arriving at work by remitting that monthly car payment. While a donation to Greenpeace may alleviate some guilt, it does not offer a measurement of how well we are doing compared to our neighbors in the same way that purchasing the latest in consumer technology or a gas-guzzling SUV allows us to feel "superior" to our neighbors.

No matter the threat to the environment, we take little time to seek out and create accurate, updated information that can pragmatically inform us and move us to ethical action. Although we might believe that we must somehow take both ecological and social concerns fully into account, we mostly just live our everyday lives. Nothing—the social, the ecological, our everyday lives—is problematized. We generally operate with the illusion that the ecological, no matter how damaged, will continue to sustain the social indefinitely. That is, until we encounter what we can no longer deny.

Collective critical reflection about and action upon everyday lived tensions such as those described could be a vital process toward expanding the field of environmental adult education (EAE) beyond "preaching to the choir" or the privileged few. As Krall (1994) states: "We can speak to each other, but conversation is not enough. Nor is a critical self-consciousness that allows us to question ourselves and open ourselves to the questions of others sufficient. . . . We must acknowledge the tension between the rights and responsibilities of the individual and the community and the maintenance or restoration of integrity and health of the Earth" (p. 233).

In the project described here, the women participating acknowledged this and other tensions in their everyday lives, although they also questioned what moved them to action and who should hold responsibility for protecting the environment.

The SWEEPE Project

The Supporting Women for Economics, the Environment, and Popular Education (SWEEPE) project—a tentative group name proposed by one member—arose in part from an exploration of the tension between inaction and action to protect the environment. The longer the tension continues, the more pertinent the question of how and if like-minded women who are schooled in and/or practicing adult and popular education acknowledge and live this tension.

This project, involving group exploration and the collective development of environmental awareness, was initiated over the six-month period April to September 2001. Seven women involved in adult and popular education were invited by the instructor to participate in what one woman later called a "dialogue to social action" group. The course instructor chose these women because each had expressed a feeling of urgency to direct attention to women and the environment. The women all had participated in and created or co-created self- and group projects and actions central to environmental adult education. They are the kind of women who are often the early adopters of paradigmatic change.

For the purpose of describing this project, the following definitions will be used. "Local" means a northwestern U.S. coastal college town. "Environment" means the totality of surroundings, both social (particularly as related with women) *and* ecological (usually named "the environment" or "nature") (Krall, 1994). "Women" means mostly European-American, privileged, well-schooled females with many "ist" (environmentalist, spiritualist, feminist/womynist, activist) leanings, but who are not, of course, representative of all women. "Educators" mean these women with their past and current, paid and unpaid, adult educative roles ranging from work in English as a second language (ESL) and adult basic education (ABE) to ecotheology, gay liberation, and indigenous environmental education.

Of the seven women, two are involved in formal and informal adult and popular education in the local community and were not students during the study. One is an adult literacy administrator with a love of movement, women, and the woods. The other is a university teacher and coordinator with popular and adult education experience, especially around spirituality and Central American issues.

The other five women—a university worker, volunteer coordinator, activist, and two teachers—were recently or nearly graduated students in the adult education program at a local university. Four of the five women were enrolled in a class called Current Issues in Adult Education, which was offered in spring 2001. Students could choose to participate for course credit. The fifth woman, a recent program graduate, entered the group after it began at the behest of one of the student members.

Project Workings. The project included three formal meetings, one informal meeting, and ten class meetings as well as individual follow-up interviews held in a space of each woman's choosing. Meeting discussion centered on the connections between and among each woman's sharing from the first meeting as well as the *starters,* and *stoppers* influencing both the connections and their environmental awareness. Starters are those things that move one to act to improve the health of the environment. Stoppers are those things that prevent one from action, such as fear of losing a job.

The women participated in two additional activities that became tools for their exploration. The first was the individual writing of what was called a socioenvironmental autobiography. Here, the women reviewed life events critical to the development of their socioenvironmental herstories. During the first group meeting, they shared at least one incident critical to leading them to their present state of activism. The second activity was participation in at least one group social action, designed to demonstrate the need to protect the environment, scheduled before Earth Day 2002. This arose from an unspoken initial and later revised belief that coincided with E. Lindeman's 1945 article in the *Journal of Educational Sociology* (cited in Cranton, 1994): "All successful adult education groups sooner or later become social action groups" (p. 137).

Observations. Initially, the graduate students took this project on as a refreshing change, an opportunity to work more closely with content they cared about and women they appreciated in a process they co-created. The two community women decided to "help out in this interesting project" but only during this time-specific period. All seven women fit this project into their already overextended lives.

At the first meeting, the women tentatively yet openly shared searing pain they had experienced that shaped their awareness about the environment. Their stories revealed literal and figurative "rape" of their personal environment (the body) and the socioecological habitat with its inhabitants. The group also shared experiences of pure joy, childhood "safe" green spaces, and companion animals that befriended them or they befriended.

At the second meeting, the women approached their work—to develop connections—with vitality and respect amid the beginning of deconstruction of the andocentric and patriarchal paradigm. Two general categories of connection emerged: systemic power over sociopolitical, cultural, and economic forces, and power dynamics within groups and interpersonal exchanges. These were described later as starters and stoppers in the follow-up interviews.

The third meeting consisted of the discussion of whether or not to continue as a group, and for what purposes, as well as a sharing of resources. This "community women-environment audit," as one woman called it, ranged from reports about the Green Party and city council and community group activities to an invitation to witness in protest the visit of a nationally prominent homophobe. The women then decided to view and discuss relevant films. There seemed to be a prevailing sense that this group just might transform into a space where, as one woman said, "I can become who I really am and want to become, and to cohabit a society, an environment, I want to be part of." She echoed M. P. Follett ([1918] 1998): "There is 'no' society thought of vaguely as the mass of people around us. I am always in relation not to society but to some concrete group. . . . Practically, 'society' is for every one of us a number of groups. . . . The vital relation of the individual to the world is through his [sic] groups; they are the potent factors in shaping our lives" (p. 20).

These relations between the women and their social groups, and hence society, were a recurrent theme in the follow-up interviews. Not surprisingly, as they honed in on the personal, the nebulous women-education-environment focus ceased to be too large to get their minds and hearts around.

Patterns of SWEEPE

Throughout the project, emergent patterns were tracked and coded. As LaChapelle (1992) states: "Each being has its own *li*—its own pattern. . . . If one could feel the entire universe, then one could see how the *li* of each part fits with the *li* of the whole; but no one can know the entire universe. All we can really learn to know fully is our own place on earth where we live. We can learn to recognize the patterns which underlie the seeming chaos" (pp. 234–235).

Overall, two patterns—attending and ritual—evolved from the "seeming chaos" that in this project appeared as deeply ambivalent tensions regarding barely acknowledged, often hidden, and seemingly incompatible competing and conflicting interests.

For example, one woman shared her constant tension with her decision to eat salmon, an endangered species, which fed her taste and appetite. She improved her personal health by passing a blood test for anemia, yet she was torn with her complicity in the demise of a species that for eons has been central to the social *and* ecological place she inhabited. Other tensions included solo driving to an environmental meeting because of "lack of time" when bicycling, bussing, or walking were options; eating easily accessible meat and fast food so another activity could be included in a frantic, fast-paced, overly crowded day; buying unnecessary but "comforting" objects; and taking daily long, hot showers, frequenting golf courses, and stringing up electric holiday lights. None of these tensions seems significant by itself; however, it is the aggregate of the tensions that throws life and the environment into chaos.

Pattern One: Attending. The women repeatedly brought attention to nonhuman sentient beings, including the earth, with respect and care during group meetings and each follow-up interview. Tales of mourning, such as vain attempts to aid an injured, exploited animal, joined with tales of reunion and purification, including honoring a natural place that kept the spirit alive during troubled times as well as tales of communication with other species, such as companion animals, and ongoing relations with the ecological wilderness and the wilderness in themselves.

This attention extended to the women of the group but in a different way than that of paying attention, which "turns a gift into an economic transaction" (Bateson, 1994, p. 109), or the enforced attention due to a crisis, which "interrupts all else that we're doing and rivets us on someone else's agenda which we didn't agree to" (Hoagland, 1990, p. 271). It was more like the attending of which Hoagland speaks: "When we attend someone or something, we focus on them or it and hence we give them or it our energy. . . . Our channels of communication are open and we are sending and receiving energy. . . . Being able to attend each other means we can steady each other and ourselves as we face our individual situations. And that steadiness, I want to suggest, is what will help us actively resist oppression" (pp. 127–129).

Perhaps due in part to the developing steadiness in the group and because there might become "a safe space to begin to disagree," the women began to concern themselves with attending their differences. They questioned themselves: Did the ritual offend a woman with a secular, native, or Christian sensibility? Is racism the reason for one woman's absence? Did no one participate in an invitational activity because the focus was not one accepted by the women? Did they go too far/far enough during a U.S. Independence Day flag action designed to raise attention to the corporatization of the United States?

These women struggled with the understanding that real and perceived, suppressed or denied difference acts as a stopper to what Krall (1994) says is the "fundamental point of discourse": "to clarify the right of the individual to actualize her or his potential within community for the social and ecological good" (p. 233). Actualizing the self *and* her social groups for the "good of all" is what one woman called her central tension or stopper. Later, she stated this could also be her most powerful starter. She was seeking to experience *autokoenony,* which Hoagland (1990) describes as one "who is both separate and related, a self which is neither autonomous nor dissolved: a self in community who is one among many" (p. 12). Hoagland explains that the "benefit of perceiving our selves as one among many encourages a unique sense of self as well as an understanding and real appreciation of difference" (p. 239). This dynamic is important because the competition between the self and larger groups is lessened as "the process of interacting with one another (encountering difference and so expanding our horizons, delighting in agreement and so conspiring) does not take the form of placing one self over and against another self" (p. 237).

A call for experiencing autokoenony or self in community was directly or indirectly central in six of the seven interviews. For example: "When it comes to women and the environment, I want my voice heard, not in front of or behind others, but in concert with many other voices." Two frequently mentioned "starters" to building responses to protect the environment and experiencing autokoenonic moments were the perceptions and realities of legitimacy and credibility by "powerful others" as well as the less often mentioned "courage to risk expressing who I am and what I'm about instead of worrying about fitting in."

The SWEEPE women who were enrolled in the class experienced what can happen when expression is courageously attempted in an institutional setting. The professor's support for a pervasive, repeated focus on women and the environment in every class activity created resistance from other students in the class. This gave the SWEEPE women yet another opportunity to develop their awareness as they experienced and examined the unintended consequences of multiple voices legitimating the environment and women in a conventional institutional space.

When these women returned to the SWEEPE group, they wanted, as one woman said, to "lick our wounds." They needed to experience something different from the "too much, too soon, too strange" response in the class space of unsettling, shifting power dynamics and contested talk time. To attempt this, they co-created a way, a ritual.

Pattern Two: Awakening Awareness Through Ritual. The women followed up on an initiation of ritual at their first meeting in which creation of a safe, accepting atmosphere was purposefully attempted through intent, process, and activities. The rituals drew heavily on the traditions brought to the group by the one Native American student and on rituals learned from Christianity and goddess worship. They continued to integrate into their meetings ritual that usually involved synchronized body movement, breathing, and sounds. These fifteen-minute rituals seemed to clear, open, and focus their energy. They deepened their capacity for more careful, honest communication, to "quit staying in the head, as this is what got us [women, environment] into this mess in the first place." Another woman said: "Even in this hierarchical place [university campus setting], I felt my spirit begin to awaken."

The women also evolved what for them became a second ritual: the continual sharing of information about resources, events, and incidents relevant to this project. This information sharing might have evolved from the women's academic setting, as the project was seeded in a graduate course. Even though the women were "overwhelmed with information," they repeatedly chose to seek out and share the facts of "what's really happening" using sources *they* selected. At first, this consisted of books, websites, and announcements of speakers and upcoming events. National, international, transgovernmental, and private-sector policy reports; pending legislation; or theoretical and philosophical writings about ecological feminism were rarely part of their sharing.

Later, viewing and discussing environmental films became the primary group activity, along with information sharing and social gatherings that continued beyond the formal project period. The women's interest in this educational tool for themselves and others came about from a class assignment. They experienced the power of visual representation in *Pow Wow Highway* (1987) with its striking visual contradictions of the beauty and ugliness of life on a North Dakota reservation. This allowed the contributor to share understandings of the conceptual interconnections between and among class, indigenous, and ecological oppression. That the same participant had successfully shared the film clips with her adult students in a well-received ABE class activity sparked the women's motivation to experience this themselves.

Working Conclusions

The SWEEPE experience, at least in part, became a space of paying attention. For the four SWEEPE women enrolled in the graduate course, the power of the instructor to issue grades and to enforce compliance with course requirements (no matter how widely interpreted) clearly located the SWEEPE experience within the classroom. Simultaneously, however, a popular education model emerged from the sharing of resources and the media contributions, both of which required critical analysis and the formation of connections. SWEEPE as a whole also moved closer to a popular education model with the assignment of a socioenvironmental autobiography followed by group sharing of critical incidents.

SWEEPE, like many environmental adult educative groups, may spark questions for practitioners and researchers to explore the development and continuation of SWEEPE-like groups. Was its short history as a "dialogue to social action group" the result of too much adherence to classroom expectations? Was timing an issue for the four graduate students who tired of anything that required social requirements with an agenda not of their making? Is SWEEPE successful if the numerous post-SWEEPE organizations continue for these women and hence society?

Environmental adult educators would do well to wrestle with questions like these and discern how potential and current EAE might respond. Multiple forms of EAE could be generated that match potential and current needs for EAE. This could be translated into more participation by more people. Also, in this way, EAE as a relatively newly recognized educational phenomena might contribute to short-circuiting hierarchical canonical strangleholds.

To encourage women educators' environmental awareness and participation, holding space open for the above combination of elements and questions may well be a necessity. This does not mean throwing out the past or system elements already in place. It does mean aligning values, purposes, and activities more congruently with current realities. It does eventually mean "unlearning," a letting go and teaching others to let go of unnecessary and inappropriate beliefs and desired outcomes. This would entail the acknowledgment and practice of self- and group reflexivity that makes tensions between beliefs and daily-life choices transparent and begins to take unintended consequences into account.

For example, a lack of reflexivity and nonattention to unintended consequences and mixed motives on the part of the project initiator led to an initial request for a group social action. This unnecessary expectation and inappropriate outcome was based on the belief that the indicator of a successful adult education group was its development into a social action group (E. Lindeman, cited in Cranton, 1994). This could have meant multiple, publicly visible SWEEPE group activities such as the one held on the U.S. Independence Day, 2001. Further, wonderfully organic spin-offs such as the following would have been ignored, negated, or minimized:

- Personal sitting with, and attention to, the women-environment-education nexus that at times erupted with tensions arising from new awareness of complicity with "agendas that work to destroy everything and everyone I care about."
- Local ecological projects such as stream restoration in which three SWEEPE women involved themselves.
- The participation of two SWEEPE members in an annual eagle census.
- The study of nonviolence with its increasing relevance to environmental adult education. One SWEEPE woman, in continuing her study as a personal life project, attracted another SWEEPE woman to take this on in her life.

- Participation by three SWEEPE women at a 2002 environmental film festival. The group as a whole then talked about creating a local environmental film festival, much like an annual local human rights film festival planned in part by one SWEEPE woman.

There is strong evidence that there will be groups similar to SWEEPE in these women's lives. It is likely that conventional institutional representatives will not understand or accept as legitimate such results as the ones listed. Indeed, people on this path may be often misunderstood and punished. And it is likely that environmental adult educators who do not warmly welcome results considered desirable by women in SWEEPE-like groups will not succeed in attracting women like them to their projects.

The integration and wise use of direct connection with social *and* ecological concerns; ritual; accurate, updated, accessible information about what matters; and attention to the sensory meaning, including kinesthetic as well as visual concerns, the socioenvironmental autobiography, and the development and sharing of incidents critical to a woman's *herstory* seem to have concretely formed the environmental awareness of SWEEPE women.

To date, direct connection with the ecology is the frequent choice of the SWEEPE women, who, as one woman put it, "feel so very disconnected from the earth." Only the Native American woman, who is already connected with international, national, and regional socioenvironmental groups, appears to live her social *and* ecological awareness in any sustained, systemic way. Currently, the SWEEPE women are organizing or participating in peace actions.

The SWEEPE women would not need to drop any or all of their current life roles in order to continue to make decisions to grow awareness and perhaps take action as individuals or as group members. In this way, they could continue to make individual decisions to choose to take action motivated by concern. Largely because of their lives in an individualist, materialist, capitalist society, they continue to be wary of long-term time commitments. Still, they often show their concern through short-term actions including attendance at a public meeting, communication to officials, or making monetary contributions.

Yet the SWEEPE women, as demonstrated by their attention, language, and autokoenony, are not at all satisfied with lives and a world that do not at least attempt to fully encompass the social and ecological realms. They would, in all likelihood, agree with Thompson (1980) when she wrote: "As so often in the past, the future of adult education is still one of uncertainty (p. 221). It should be clear . . . that whatever the outcome, 'more of the same' is not, in our opinion, the way forward" (p. 222). The way forward for environmental adult education involves the use of critical reflection about and action upon everyday lived tensions along with increased autokoenonic moments.

References

Bateson, M. C. *Peripheral Visions: Learning Along the Way.* New York: HarperCollins, 1994.

Cranton, P. *Understanding and Promoting Transformative Learning: A Guide for Educators of Adults.* San Francisco: Jossey-Bass, 1994.

Follett, M. P. *The New State: Group Organization and the Solution of Popular Government.* University Park: Pennsylvania State University Press, 1998. (Originally published 1918.)

Hoagland, S. L. *Lesbian Ethics: Toward New Values.* Palo Alto, Calif.: Institute of Lesbian Studies, 1990.

Krall, F. R. *Ecotone: Wayfaring on the Margins.* Albany: State University of New York Press, 1994.

LaChapelle, D. "Not Laws of Nature But Li (Pattern) of Nature." In M. Oelschlaeger (ed.), *The Wilderness Condition: Essays on Environment and Civilization.* San Francisco: Sierra Club Books, 1992.

Thompson, J. L. *Adult Education for a Change.* London: Hutchinson, 1980.

LEE KARLOVIC is the former editor and publisher of The Space Between *and director of an intercultural women's center in Costa Rica as well as an adult education and ESL program in Korea.*

KATHRYN PATRICK is an administrator and instructor at Western Washington University.

7

Strategies for developing critical and active environmental literacy in adults are discussed in the context of developing and participating in the social practices likely to change the way our societies think about and act on ecological issues.

Words for the World: Creating Critical Environmental Literacy for Adults

Ralf St. Clair

What does it mean to be literate? As with so many educational questions, the answer depends upon whom you ask. Some would say that literacy is the ability to read and write, to use the tools of written language in an instrumental way. Others would say that literacy also concerns the critical application of these tools to understanding the world. Action is often a component of this second perspective—the idea that critical understanding will lead to activities to transform the status quo. When the metaphor of literacy is applied to areas other than written language, the same issues are carried over. For example, does health literacy mean understanding the label on a bottle of pills, or does it include a critical awareness of the ways in which the Western medical system pathologizes us?

My position is that literacy is more than an instrumental activity. Literacy must be critical and active, focused on making a difference. In this chapter I discuss what it would mean to bring this perspective to environmental literacy education. I begin by discussing the perspectives on environmental literacy developed in formal education settings. While much of this work is useful, it must be developed further to be appropriate for adult activists. I make a number of suggestions about this development and sketch a tentative portrait of critical and activist environmental literacy education for adults. I close with a case study demonstrating such an approach in action.

The Roots of Environmental Literacy

The notion of environmental literacy is generally agreed to have emerged from the work of Charles E. Roth (1968) in the late 1960s. Roth's defini-

NEW DIRECTIONS FOR ADULT AND CONTINUING EDUCATION, no. 99, Fall 2003 © Wiley Periodicals, Inc.

tion of the term developed over twenty-five years of work in the area, and in the early 1990s he explained: "Environmental literacy is essentially the capacity to perceive and interpret the relative health of environmental systems and take appropriate action to maintain, restore, or improve the health of those systems. . . . Environmental literacy should be defined . . . in terms of observable behaviors. That is, people should be able to demonstrate in some observable form what they have learned—their knowledge of key concepts, skills acquired, disposition towards issues, and the like" (cited in Disinger and Roth, 1992, p. 2).

In many ways this represents a classic, and formal, definition. Another, apparently simpler way of explaining environmental literacy is to view it as the ability to ask "what's next?" when making decisions likely to impact the environment (Orr, 1992). This deceptively simple question depends upon individuals and groups being willing to develop the ability to think through the long-term effects of decisions made in the short term. For example, the positive and negative connotations of asking "What's next?" can be seen in considering personal transportation options in North America. If the societal trend toward bigger and more fuel-hungry hydrocarbon-powered vehicles continues, the "What's next?" question leads to a gloomy prognosis. Emphasizing alternative methods of transportation such as public transport, bicycles, and walking leads to a far more optimistic conclusion. If municipal officials were required to commute by public transport, for example, local residents could expect remarkable improvements in the bus service!

The term *environmental literacy* implies that environmental knowledge and the action it sustains are a specialized application of more general literacy skills, or that at least there is a substantial overlap between written-word literacy and environmental literacy. According to UNESCO (1990), "environmental literacy is no small part of effective, functional literacy, indeed, of the very essentials for a nation's sustainable development" (p. 2). This approach subsumes environmental literacy within functional literacy—the minimum degree of participation in literacy practices necessary to function within a society. In other words, to be competent as a citizen would involve recognizing the state of environmental systems and being prepared to address problems within them. This is a fascinating perspective that truly places environmental awareness at the center of education and citizenship. Instead of the ability to read a bus timetable (International Adult Literacy Survey, 2002), the mathematical component of functional literacy could be represented as awareness of the implications of varying transport policies upon atmospheric degradation—a fundamental change in the way we currently conceive basic literacy practices.

Environmental literacy holds enormous potential for radically changing the way environmental issues are conceived. The emphasis on action as the ultimate outcome and the suggestion that environmental literacy should be considered as basic—and universally desirable—as reading and writing argue for a reconceptualization of the way citizens approach the world, and what constitutes their most fundamental and most important interests.

The Four R's: Reading, wRiting, aRithmetic, enviRonment

Even though the topic of this chapter is environmental literacy for adults, it is useful to build on the resources for, and approaches to, environmental literacy developed in the K-12 arena. Despite the variety found within these resources, there are two commonly held principles. The first is the belief that environmental education must lead to action to be considered effective. The second is that environmental literacy requires a high level of scientific knowledge. Each of these principles requires some consideration.

One educator helpfully lays out six attributes of the kind of education that can lead to environmental literacy (Orr, 1992):

- Recognition that all education is environmental education
- Acknowledgment of the complexity of ecological issues and the impossibility of addressing them through a single discipline or department
- Promotion of education as a "dialogue with place" bearing the characteristics of a good conversation
- Acceptance that the process of education is as important as the content
- Inclusion of experience in the natural world as an essential component
- Enhancement of the learner's competence with natural systems

There are a number of other such lists (Coppola, 1999; Athman and Monroe, 2001), and all share an orientation toward learner empowerment and action as the final measure of program effectiveness. This orientation supports the development of critical approaches to environmental literacy by emphasizing the notion that asking about the implications of current structures is the cornerstone of competence in environmental literacy.

In practice, the emphasis on critical thought is often diluted by inclusion of other components. The Illinois Department of Natural Resources (2002), for example, suggests: "To be effective, environmental education programs should include subjects related to (1) knowledge of environmental processes and systems, including the Earth as a physical system, the living environment, humans and their societies, and environment and society, (2) questioning and analysis skills, (3) environmental issues investigation skills, (4) decision and citizenship skills, and (5) personal and civic responsibility" (p. 6).

While this approach makes reference to critical skills such as questioning and decision making, the first point highlights knowledge of environmental processes and systems—a huge and generic category. Within the formal education system, environmental literacy most frequently finds a home within science education, explaining the almost universal assumption within environmental literacy resources that more than commonsense knowledge is needed. This approach is built upon the assumption that critical exploration of environmental information requires at least a working understanding of the principles of scientific data collection and analysis. An example is the commonly used phrase "NOx emissions" widely accepted among the environmental community. Knowing that this represents a chemical formula for a smog-producing compound of nitrogen and oxygen and that one of its main sources is vehicle exhaust requires relatively advanced scientific knowledge. As I will discuss in more length later in this chapter, while this highly scientific approach may be desirable in formal education settings, it is important to be cautious about assuming that environmental literacy always depends on in-depth understanding of environmental science.

A second implication of the emphasis on scientific understanding is that it enshrines Western science as the primary means for humans to engage with the environment. There are many alternative ways of looking at the relationship between our species and nature, and it seems ironic to promote the perspective leading to the ecological crisis as the perspective most critical to its solution (Spretnak, 1993). If critical thought and action are indeed central components of environmental literacy, surely critical reflection upon the worldview represented by Western science is one of the most fundamental and potentially insightful aspects of education for environmental literacy. Science cannot be accepted as a neutral endeavor made to serve more or less desirable ends, but must be reevaluated as to its inherent assumptions about nature and the place of humans.

The importance of recognizing environmental literacy as a human—and social—concern is reflected in the report of a research project setting out to identify the social science concepts necessary to understand environmental issues (McKeown-Ice and Dendinger, 2000). Sixty-three such concepts were identified. Item 39 states: "All activities have a cost, and someone in this generation or future generations will pay monetarily or in intangible ways," and item 58 states: "Individuals are responsible for their own decisions and actions, and there are consequences to those actions" (p. 41). These two concepts are particularly interesting because they appear to privilege individualistic and economically centered understandings of the world. The notion of costs being either monetary or intangible is interesting. What of costs that are tangible but not monetary, such as the health consequences of environmental decisions? While the philosophy of environmental literacy is global and holistic (Orr, 1992), concrete examples of curricula often collapse back into individualistic and economic concerns. To the degree that they do collapse in this way, they counteract the push for critical action at the center of environmental literacy.

The challenge for adult educators interested in environmental literacy is to retain the valuable and motivating insights of the field while stepping away from those likely to be counterproductive. As in all forms of literacy, the path toward critical engagement with the world and the word winds its way between many potential complexities.

Shaping Adult Education for Environmental Literacy

To date, most discussion about environmental literacy (and most of the resources) concentrates on schoolchildren, but there are important reasons why adults should also be given the opportunity to become environmentally literate. These include the following (National Institute of Adult Continuing Education, 1993):

- There is insufficient time to wait for younger generations to mature before environmental action is taken.
- Environmental education must be lifelong.
- Understanding of environmental issues changes over time.
- Adults must change if the environmental education of children is to have credibility.
- Environmental change requires engagement of the widest possible range of people.

Perhaps the strongest rationale, from an environmental educator's perspective, is the lack of time for our societies to react to the challenges raised by such issues as global warming and deforestation. People hoping to develop environmental literacy programs have a number of strategic decisions to make and issues to explore. Several of these are directly educational, but others are related to the wider social context of such endeavors. Any education for social change, including the critical projects I view as the most valuable examples of adult education (Horton, 1990; Freire, 1972), require educators to engage with their context to understand the effects of, and reactions to, their endeavors.

One of the most important issues to think through is the extent to which environmental literacy education for adults addresses an educational problem (Mager and Pipe, 1970). There is some evidence that it takes more than education for people to become committed to environmental action. One study of environmental activists in Kentucky, USA, and Norway (Chawla, 1999) found that education was mentioned as a source of commitment by only 38 percent of overall respondents. Experience of natural areas (77 percent), family (64 percent), and participation in environmental or outdoors organizations (55 percent) were mentioned significantly more frequently. Negative experiences—for example, the destruction of a loved wilderness area—were mentioned by 39 percent of respondents. The implication of this study is that formal environmental literacy education may not be a strong precursor of action when considered in isolation. Chawla's research failed to address whether informal self-education or group study played a part in developing commitment to action, though it seems reasonable to assume that most people had at least some element of these activities in their preparation for activism. The point of this, for environmental adult educators, is not that environmental literacy is beyond the scope of education to develop, but rather that educators should explicitly recognize and build upon the experiences of learners when developing programs and materials. Environmental literacy is a resource for linking *experience* to *action* and can never be a substitute for either.

Another interesting issue is the question of scientific knowledge mentioned earlier in this chapter. The assumption that environmental literacy requires a high, and relatively uncommon, level of training in scientific thinking has the potential to create an elite of environmentally literate citizens and a mass of people who either follow along or are completely excluded from informed environmental action. Ecofeminist writers in particular have done a good job of identifying and addressing this problem. Spretnak (1993) argues that the assumption that the human is separate from the natural world—a fundamental of Western science since the time of Bacon—tends to lead to isolated and harmful judgments about environmental issues. Instead, these ecofeminist theorists suggest there is a need to develop connective ways to look at the environment, based on what humans share with each other and the natural world rather than what sets us apart: "A new science should never lose sight of the fact that we are part of Nature, that we have a body, that we are dependent on Mother Earth, that we are born by women, and that we die. It should never lead to the abdication of our senses as a source of knowledge" (Mies, 1993, p. 52).

In educational terms, this means always working toward localization of environmental issues, a strategy borrowed from other forms of political literacy (Freire, 1972). For example, people working to decrease use of polluting personal transport in their neighborhood do not necessarily need to know about speciation. It makes more sense to begin with the basic knowledge most relevant to the real-life problem—gas and particulate pollution. This is not to suggest that scientific knowledge is necessarily trivial, but it is only one resource for action, to be considered alongside experience, ethics, political interests, and other vital concerns. Adults tend to be more motivated to learn and to act by things they care about rather than by abstract concerns, and one critical role of educators is to show people why they should care about the environment before expecting them to acknowledge its importance and begin to build environmental literacy.

Another aspect of the emphasis on scientific knowledge is the concealment of diversity. When environmental literacy is lodged unproblematically within a discourse of conventional science it argues for a universal approach to nature, based upon one "best," or most rigorous, way of seeing the world. But the way people understand science and nature are inevitably and fundamentally shaped by their gender, ethnicity, religious background, socioeconomic status, geographical location, and so on. Any single approach is likely to founder on these dimensions of diversity if they are not recognized as strengths and brought into environmental literacy in a meaningful way. For example, the higher cost makes it unlikely that people living in poverty will ever choose food made from non–genetically modified organisms, however well they are educated on the issues. Also, some of the assumptions behind environmental literacy, evolution for example, may contradict religious teachings and cultural narratives. Finding a way to connect across diversity is both difficult and essential to the creation of sustainable environmental literacy.

The final issue to be considered is whether a social movement exists within which the potential for action can be realized. Environmental literacy tends to operate on the assumption that knowledge, and perhaps experience, lead inevitably to environmental activism. In fact, the link is obscure for any social movement (Vandenabeele and Wildemeersch, 1998). A complex combination of social and individual forces bear on the choices we make, and the temptation to believe that knowledge is sufficient by itself to convince people that responsible environmental choices are correct and cause them to act in specific ways must be resisted (Salmon, 2000). Horton (1990) argues that adult education is not sufficient for social change, even though it may be necessary. Political action relies upon a social movement to pressure for change once people are aware of the importance of the cause. Educators interested in environmental literacy have to ensure their work links with, and contributes to, local, national, and global social movements committed to environmental issues.

These concerns lead to the emergence of a number of central strategies for the development of adult environmental literacy education. Educators may benefit from spending time with learners working out exactly what issue they will address together, and based on that, what resources of scientific knowledge would be helpful. In addition, forming alliances with social movements and other groups interested in similar issues would also be constructive. The curriculum, however loosely defined, must include elements of the learner's experience and attempt to recognize diversity as widely as possible. Finally, it is important to decide what environmental literacy means to educators and learners, and what kind of outcome will result from the educational process. By applying these strategies, educators will localize environmental literacy, rendering it relevant and motivating for participants, and ensure the incorporation of critical issues from their lives.

Environmental Literacy in Action

An example of critical environmental literacy education with adults can help to make these issues clearer. The Center for Health, Environment, and Justice (CHEJ, originally the Citizen's Clearinghouse for Hazardous Waste) was established in Arlington, Virginia, in 1980 (Newman, 1994). One of the founders is Lois Gibbs, formerly a leader of efforts to address the environmental effects of Love Canal, the twenty-one thousand tons of buried chemical waste lying below her community of Niagara Falls, New York. CHEJ exists to support grassroots initiatives: "CHEJ believes in environmental justice, the principle that people have the right to a clean and healthy environment regardless of their race or economic standing. Our experience has shown that the most effective way to win environmental justice is from the bottom up through community organizing and empowerment. When local citizens come together and take an organized, unified stand, they can hold industry and government accountable and work towards a healthy, environmentally sustainable future" (Center for Health, Environment, and Justice [website], 2003).

A good example of their work is the support they gave to Los Coyotes, a Californian Native American band in 1991 (Newman, 1994). A development company that wished to establish a solid waste landfill on tribal land produced a lease said to be signed by the tribal chairman. The lease both waived the band's sovereign immunity (leaving them open to prosecution if things went wrong) and encumbered their lands for twenty-five years. Members of the band contacted CHEJ in search of information and strategies to be used in preparing their response to this development.

"[CHEJ] sent information both on the company and on landfills and began to talk them through the issue. We wanted to discover what their concerns were, who was making the decisions, and how other members felt about the proposal. . . . In thinking through the issues and analyzing their own strengths, the members saw they had most power with their own people, through their own local political processes" (Newman, 1994, p. 53).

The approach taken by CHEJ begins by addressing the extent to which this is an educational problem. Information is a vital resource, but it is accompanied by the beginnings of a political process of analyzing the workings of power in the community, and working out how to call on that power. CHEJ strategies go far beyond conventional constructions of environmental education in order to reach the goal of stopping the landfill, recognizing that effective action requires engagement with the political realities of local community. The scientific information that was provided was closely targeted to the issue and aligned with other sources of knowledge, such as the band's relationship with its lands. In addition, CHEJ put the Los Coyotes band members in touch with other organizations fighting landfills or representing Native American groups in their struggle for land rights.

The issues laid out in the previous section are well addressed in the CHEJ model. Rather than attempting to impose a vast amount of environmental education upon a group concerned with one central issue, CHEJ worked to localize the sphere of action. This meant both bringing their own resources to bear in a highly contextualized manner and also encouraging local people to explore the resources they had available in the community. The success of this process in the case of Los Coyotes was due as much to the concrete, situated approach of environmental education—the localization of environmental literacy—as to any specialized knowledge contributed by the national organization.

Conclusion

The arguments in this chapter reflect an active, situated, and critical way of applying the metaphor of literacy to environmental issues. Instead of viewing literacy as a state attained through the ingestion of sufficient knowledge, I have argued that it represents a set of social practices (Barton, Hamilton, and Ivanic, 2000). In the case of environmental literacy for adults, this means developing and participating in the social practices likely to change the way our societies think about and act upon ecological issues. Literacy is a powerful metaphor that contributes a great deal to thinking through the question of what each of us can contribute for a more just and more sustainable way of life for the planetary community.

References

Athman, J. A., and Monroe, M. C. "Elements of Effective Environmental Education Programs." In A. Fedler (ed.), *Defining Best Practices in Boating, Fishing, and Stewardship Education.* Alexandria, Va.: Recreational Boating and Fishing Foundation, 2001.

Barton, D., Hamilton, M., and Ivanic, R. *Situated Literacies: Reading and Writing in Context.* London: Routledge, 2000.

Center for Health, Environment, and Justice. [http://www.chej.org/about.html]. Feb. 18, 2003.

Chawla, L. "Life Paths into Effective Environmental Action." *Journal of Environmental Education,* 1999, *31*(1), 15–26.

Coppola, N. "Greening the Technological Curriculum: A Model for Environmental Literacy." *Journal of Technology Studies,* 1999, *25,* 39–46.

Disinger, J. F., and Roth, C. E. *Environmental Literacy.* Columbus, Ohio: ERIC Clearinghouse for Science, Mathematics, and Environmental Education, 1992. (ED 351 201)

Freire, P. *Pedagogy of the Oppressed.* Harmondsworth, England: Penguin Books, 1972.

Horton, M., with Kohl, J., and Kohl, H. *The Long Haul: An Autobiography.* New York: Doubleday, 1990.

Illinois Department of Natural Resources. "Environmental Literacy for Illinois." [http://dnr.state.il.us/entice/partners/ELIL.htm]. Oct. 25, 2002.

International Adult Literacy Survey. "Canadian Adult Literacy Database." [http://www.nald.ca/nls/ials/introduc.htm]. Feb. 18, 2002.

McKeown-Ice, R., and Dendinger, R. "Socio-Political-Cultural Foundations of Environmental Education." *Journal of Environmental Education,* 2000, *31*(4), 37–45.

Mager, R. F., and Pipe, P. *Analyzing Performance Problems.* Belmont, Calif.: Fearon, 1970.

Mies, M. "Feminist Research: Science, Violence, and Responsibility." In M. Mies and V. Shiva (eds.), *Ecofeminism* (pp. 36–54). Atlantic Highlands, N.J.: Zed Books, 1993.

National Institute of Adult Continuing Education. *Learning for the Future: Adult Learning and the Environment.* Leicester, England: National Institute of Adult Continuing Education, 1993.

Newman, P. "Killing Legally with Toxic Waste: Women and the Environment in the United States." In V. Shiva (ed.), *Close to Home: Women Connect Ecology, Health, and Development Worldwide.* Philadelphia: New Society, 1994.

Orr, D. W. *Ecological Literacy: Education and the Transition to a Postmodern World.* Albany: State University of New York Press, 1992.

Roth, C. E. "On the Road to Conservation." *Massachusetts Audubon,* June 1968, pp. 38–41.

Salmon, J. "Are We Building Environmental Literacy?" *Journal of Environmental Education,* 2000, *31*(4), 4–10.

Spretnak, C. "Critical and Constructive Contributions of Ecofeminism." In M. E. Tucker and J. A. Grim (eds.), *Worldviews and Ecology.* Lewisburg, Penn.: Bucknell University Press, 1993.

UNESCO. *Environmental Education.* Geneva: UNESCO-UNEP International Environmental Education Programme, 1990.

Vandenabeele, J., and Wildemeersch, D. "Learning for Sustainable Development: Examining Lifeworld Transformation Among Farmers." In D. Wildemeersch, M. Finger, and T. Jansen (eds.), *Adult Education and Social Responsibility.* Frankfurt, Germany: Peter Lang, 1998.

RALF ST. CLAIR is an assistant professor of adult education at Texas A&M University and director of the Texas Center for Adult Literacy and Learning.

8

This chapter explores the use of ecological language and proposes a framework for environmental lifelong learning that fosters the empowerment of people and communities in relationship to a changing environment.

Learning Environments and Environmental Education

Paul Bélanger

Environmental problems cannot be separated from the entire nexus of problems related to economic development in so-called underdeveloped and underconsuming countries and those in so-called developed, overproducing, and overconsuming countries of our postindustrial world. Moreover, environmental problems cannot be analyzed independently of collective ecological and social actions taking place around the globe. This broader vision, articulated in the Brundtland Report (World Commission on Environment and Development, 1987) and reiterated at the United Nations–sponsored Earth Summit of 1992 in Rio and the Rio+5 follow-up conference, has had a major impact on environmental education and the adult education discourse of lifelong learning.

This chapter explores the concept of the "learning environment" and environmental lifelong learning (ELL). Articulating a framework of "environmental" lifelong learning creates a contemporary vision that recognizes the important role that many adult education initiatives play within the environmental education scene. It also implies an ecological transformation of all educational practices as the combination of environment and adult education acquires new meaning through the notion of an *ecology of learning* (Orellana, 2002; Hautecoeur, 2000; Wenger, 1998; Schön, 1983). The appropriation by adult education of a concept normally used solely by biologists and environmentalists can help to create synergy between formal, nonformal, and informal education and enhance our understandings of how learning environments contain hidden curricula that influence participation and cognitive development.

Learning Environments

Many researchers have come to realize that the learning-teaching transaction cannot be improved without more knowledge about the interaction between an individual and his or her environment, about ecological approaches to perception, and about individual insights prompted and mediated by life contexts (Gibson, 1979). These ideas about the social-psychology of education come from Bronfenbrenner and Morris (1997) and others who introduced the expression *ecology of cognitive development*. Since adults operate in real-life settings with real-life implications, they also have the capacity to *experience* their environments and to learn from them. They have the capacity to reconstruct the ecologies in which they live and grow.

The notion of a *learning society,* closely associated with lifelong learning, refers not only to the diversification of learning opportunities but also to the diffuse impact of cultural environments in which adult learners find themselves at different phases of their life (Delors, 1996). On a daily basis, we experience our surroundings and neighborhood, and these affect the development of our mental concepts and representations. The managerial literature refers to a similar concept, which is often described as the *learning organization* (Senge, 1990; Watkins and Marsick, 1993; Cohen and Sproull, 1995). In literacy education, the term is known as the *literate environment* (Wagner, 2002; Olson, 1975).

The core idea at play here is that diverse cultural contexts are unevenly conducive to creative learning. Each educational activity operates in a specific cultural and institutional context that carries its own informal curriculum (Bélanger, 1995). These surroundings influence the individuals' educational aspirations, may stimulate or have an anesthetic effect on their curiosity, or may help or hinder their ability to be cognizant of environmental issues. The type of learning milieu affects the continuation of a person's learning biography (Bélanger and Tuijnman, 1997).

Work environments do not all foster creativity or function as learning organizations, neither do they all operate as "industrial democracies." Indeed, care must be taken not to mistake the business concept of the learning organization for a necessarily benign form of ecological learning. It is true that the *learning organization* focuses on the learning of employees within their workplace context, but business purposes necessarily prevail. Watkins (1995) wrote that by fostering a learning organization, the role of the human resource development practitioner is to systematically and developmentally increase the learning capacity of the organization so as to meet the challenges facing organizations. Likewise, Rothwell and Kazanas (1994) comment that the role of human resource development is "related to what the organization should do to encourage planned learning that supports business and staffing plans" (p. 1).

Unfortunately, the way the terms *ecology of learning* and even *ecological learning* are being used must also be carefully examined since examples of these terms being co-opted to describe learning topics and contexts that have little to do with the natural environment can be found in the education literature.

Care must also be taken to examine messages in the media encountered in people's daily surrounding and the type(s) of media available. As early as 1959, Raymond William recognized the influence of "the press and popular education" on the development of informal and formal learning among the adult population in diverse cultural contexts (McIlroy and Westwood, 1993). Certainly, many examples can be observed of natural symbols being used to promote corporate products and practices that are environmentally destructive.

Learning environments cannot be considered neutral. They tend to have either a repressive effect or the ability to strengthen learning and progressive initiatives to make change in society. Just as the biosphere in which human beings live is ever changeable, learning environments are not static or fixed. They may be in a state of degradation, but they may also be protected, improved, and transformed. In this sense, no educational policy can be restricted solely to educational issues. To yield their full value, educational strategies must recognize and integrate the relationship of each subject with the environment into the learning-teaching transactions. Nevertheless, much educational research tends to ignore the *institutional pedagogies* at work in different education settings (Ardoino and Lourau, 1994).

Acknowledgment of the ecology of learning requires special educational practices to catalyze the learning potentials of each environment so as to create a cultural dynamic in which the learner can live in creative tension and reflexive relationship in his or her environment. The idea, as the Swedish adult education movement leader Sven Lindqvist would say, is to "dig where you are," or as the title of the latest book by French ecologist René Dumond (2000) suggests, "ouvrez les yeux": open your eyes. Such policies require new relations to be established between educational strategies and broader cultural policies, and between people and cultural infrastructures such as urban surroundings, museums, or natural parks. In developing a "pedagogy of place," Lewicki (1997) explained how, under certain conditions, nature teaches. Indeed, nature, streets, and buildings carry informal curricula. *New pedagogies of environments* are needed to bring to life people's cultural environments, enhancing the involvement of people in the aesthetic realm of existence in the critical assessment of their daily surroundings.

An interesting example of this recent trend in the cultural domain is a study of environmental pedagogy undertaken in Tuscany, Italy, in a *laboratory for education in environmental and cultural heritage* (Orefice, 1991). Orefice explains that the systems of cognitive representation of the reality which surrounds us and the way in which this reality is organized are linked in an extremely close relationship of interdependence. The individual relationship with an environment which stimulates his expressiveness and cultural depth is surely a valuable source of learning which broadens and enhances his system of cognitive representation, with all the positive effect on the life of an individual, certainly, but also on the environment itself.

A number of local authorities around the world are developing stronger links between the various cultural infrastructures that support learning, including museums, libraries, cultural centers, ecological parks, and adult education centers (Chadwick and Stannett, 1998; Frischkopf, 1994). Urban renewal plans are being scrutinized from a cultural anthropological perspective according to their impact on the choreography of conversation (Whalen, 1992). The cultural environment of postmodern urban living structures provides opportunities for significant adult learning in the current stage and context of neoliberal modernity (Harvey, 1990). In this perspective, how ongoing globalization creates a new challenge through a deregulated commercialization of cultural life and of the public landscape can be seen. In this sense, neither environmental adult education, nor collective action can remain local: both need a global and local vision as well as local initiatives linked to global alliance and international networks.

Different environments produce discernible differences in selecting which problems are faced, and these possibilities or obstacles can in turn be transformed and reconstructed. The concept of reflexive relations to one's environment helps us grasp this new dimension. In late modernity, life contexts have become ambivalent and uncertain. We live in a *risk society* (Beck, 1999). In the context of such *reflexive modernization* (Beck, Giddens, and Lash, 1994), individuals are freed of many social structures and restraints, and they also have more space to redefine these structures because they are living in more ambivalent life contexts and times. Under certain conditions, life contexts may lead individual and collective actors to reflect on their relations to their environment and may induce them to act to transform it.

Acknowledgment of possible different reflexive relations to one's environment, and therefore the potential of people's participation in it are critical to our new vision of education. This new vision requires a major shift from transmissive toward more reflexive and transformative forms of learning (O'Sullivan, 1999; Sterling, 2001). A growing convergence in this new perspective can be observed in the work of many social constructivists. For example, the work of Lave and Wenger (1991) shows how learning occurs through a gradual process of increasingly centripetal participation in the learning ambiance of a community of practice. Learning is "not merely situated in practice," it is "an integral part of generative social practice in the lived-in world" (Lave and Wenger, 1991). Learning occurs through the participation of the subject in a community, through a process of growing involvement. Wenger (1998) explains that the transformation of insights into knowledge can take place only in a context that creates opportunities for such participation, experience, and learning.

Yet much educational research is still too often busy with established transmissive pedagogical or andragogical methods with the purpose of achieving immediate goals of skill acquisition through mechanical and repeated replication of others' performance. This kind of practice tends to limit its attention to overt teaching and educational transactions. It has difficulty with integrating the contributions of a social theory of learning. Even environmental education can sometimes forget the ecology of learning.

Environmental Lifelong Learning

Environmental education is not new. Primary and secondary education related to the environment have included teaching and learning practices regarding environmental issues, awareness-raising, promotion of ecological sensitivity practices, and skill-training in local communities, and these have been in existence since the early 1970s (Sauvé, 2001; Robottom and Hart, 1993). They originate from conferences held in the 1970s by UNESCO and the United Nations in Stockholm, Sweden; Aix-en-Provence, France; Belgrade, in the former Yugoslavia; and other initiatives by the U.N. Environmental Programs (UNEP). Today, even more space has been given to environmental education in the official curriculum of primary and secondary education.

However, progress in this domain is limited, and in spite of international consensus, it is even more limited in regions of the world where primary education itself is still far from reaching the "education for all" goals originally set in Jomtien in 1990 (UNICEF and Inter-Agency Commission, 1990) and reinforced in Dakar in 1999 (UNESCO, 1997). Environmental education initiatives have been hampered by severe financial constraints on formal schooling imposed by the structural adjustment policies of the World Bank and the International Monetary Fund during the 1980s and the 1990s.

Problematically, the attention paid to environmental adult education is even more limited due to the market-driven provision framework characteristic of so many adult education programs. To wait thirty years for the next generation to make changes that benefit the environment is unthinkable. The ecological risks are too immediate. Therefore, environmental adult education is critical. This recognition is certainly the most significant shift that could be observed at the U.N. Conference on Environment and Development (Earth Summit) in Rio de Janeiro in 1992 and in the Agenda 21 resolution that resulted from it.

Also problematic are the environmental public education interventions that target particular communities. These tend to involve one-way communication campaigns that repeat short, motivating messages on radio, newspapers, and other media. The prevailing trend seems to rely on an information-education-communication (IEC) strategy that relies on providing specific public messages able to reach people in their daily environment through product packaging inserts, door-to-door distribution of leaflets, or through outreach initiatives undertaken by nongovernmental organizations (NGOs) that organize information tables in public meeting spaces, demonstrations, and other activities. This top-down transmissive methodology is a common framework of adult environmental education worldwide. Relying on these methods precludes creating possibilities for open communication and creating spaces for people to interact. Nor does it create opportunities for integrating an individual's personal experience with newly learned knowledge. It gives people few opportunities to become involved in significant learning that could lead to individual and collective action.

The Paradox of Non-Ecological Lifelong Learning

The way environmental education has typically been conducted carries silent messages that implicitly and powerfully contradict the official curriculum and objectives of the programs. The truth and challenge of environment education programs are to be found in their makeup, in the interaction between the subjects and their environment, and in the interrelation between learners, educators, and the social and environmental milieu. The challenge is to ensure that the *media* is not betraying the *message*. Combating this hidden curriculum requires organizing learning opportunities based mainly on observing reality—that is, relying on concrete object manipulation and shared learning rather than on pure cognition and individual cognition. The challenge is to *recycle* the approaches and recognize the environment not only as the object but also as an integrally active component of any learning experience (Collins, Greeno, and Resnick, 1996).

By neglecting the experiential learning of people and the cultural impact of an individual's relationship to his or her environment, top-down unidirectional educational practices diminish people's curiosity, engagement, and creativity. Effective environmental education requires recognizing popular and grassroots knowledge.

Contradictions in environmental teaching are reflected in other areas. Time and again, we attempt to teach democracy through authoritarian transmission of knowledge about civic participation and hope to engage individuals through passive learning. We pretend to encourage autonomous behavior yet we frequently maintain a prevailing dependent teaching relationship. Similarly, management literature introducing the idea of the "learning enterprises" often stops short of examining the relationship between a learning organization and the diffused capacity for environmental initiatives. It rarely refers to or acknowledges related issues of participative democracy or corporate responsibility (Abrahamsson, 1990; Harman and Porter, 1997).

Ecological Perspectives on Environmental Lifelong Learning That Challenge the Formal Education System

The ecological conception of lifelong learning and, subsequently, our review of the paradoxical nature of current education practices suggest four key principles of an ecological reorientation of education. The first one seems self-evident, but has not yet been adequately addressed. Effective environmental education needs to take into account the environment. Significant environmental learning is not only *about* and *for* the environment but also needs to proceed *through* and *within* the environment. Relevant learning can take place only when the subject is able to relate newly acquired knowledge to his or her own experience with his or her environment.

The second principle is that programs tend to be more effective when the focus, particularly in the beginning, is on investigation of local problems and ecological risks emerging in the area. Direct engagement with concrete challenges helps people to construct a new reflective relationship with his or her life-context. In other words, it creates an optimal learning environment. Some researchers refer to this idea as a "praxis based" approach because it integrates action and reflection (Sauvé, 2001).

Environmental education, when life-rooted, inevitably carries a lifelong and life-wide dimension. Acting on this third principle tends to create a synergy between different educational and communicational experiences and the different contexts of human activities and hence of learning. Environmental learning begins early in life and develops through a built-in inner movement whereby initial positive experiences create curiosity and aspirations for continuing, enlarging, and deepening an individual's educational life. Similarly, significant learning in one context of activities is often transferred to other ones. Growing recognition of the cumulative effect of knowledge acquisition in any subject on an individual's subsequent learning biography leads to a reexamination of the cumulative relationship between the environment, health, public, and civic and vocational adult education. The "Environmental Education Plan"—adopted in Rio de Janeiro in 1992 by the parallel nongovernmental organization International Forum—proposed exactly such a process.

The fourth principle of an ecological vision of lifelong learning relates to the interlearning potential of an interacting community. Environmental education will gain by relying on the reflexive interaction taking place when people exchange perceptions about their shared environment and when they can build on the complementary contribution of their respective skills and share their problem-solving capacity. The creation of positive community and cultural feedback processes constitutes a critical condition for sustainable learning and empowerment (Sauvé, 2001).

Environmental Adult Education Initiatives

Many ongoing experiences led by peasants' movements in Europe and in Africa are situated within a framework of environmental lifelong learning (Ziaka, Robichon, and others, 2002). Studies of emerging *communities of practices* (Wenger, 1998) in environmental adult education in Latin America are now available in the literature (Orellana, 2002). Likewise, in a new project located in Chad, I have been able to observe how positive cultural feedback processes come to life. Local fishermen are being asked to tell the true story of degradation of the parts of the lake they know best, while the farmers in the area are invited to compare different irrigation and manure fertilization practices and to share their knowledge of the location of water springs. Women, the primary community workers, have the opportunity to demonstrate new practices concerning water use and to promote closer relationships between school curricula and local adult communities. Young students can learn investigation skills allowing them to inquire into local environmental issues and test ways to solve these problems. The project in Chad also gives elders in the community the space to voice their observations about the changing ecological balance and share their expertise about uses of medical plants. Local groups now have the chance to make local inquiries.

In this kind of emancipatory learning environment, researchers and experts are being asked first to listen to the knowledge of local learning communities and only then to offer relevant knowledge and training in soil sciences, forestry, or fishery practices that are based in rigorous biophysical studies. This project was imagined and animated by an African environmental archeologist, Dr. N'Gaba Waye, and it is slowly coming to fruition despite difficult conditions.

Precisely because environmental adult learning is directly grounded in immediate problems and the expressed needs of individuals living within a sociocultural-economic context, educators must participate in real-world activities and to work with local people to create concrete, constructive action. Alternative environmental adult education leads to changes in educational practices by dealing with both the cognitive and affective dimensions of genuine learning, by allowing for transfer of knowledge from children to parents and vice-versa, and by allowing actors external to the community to intervene and relate scientific knowledge to current, local issues in a way that respects local knowledge and peoples. In this perspective, the emergence of an *ecological vision* of environmental lifelong learning over the last ten years may create a unique vision for the entire education enterprise.

Conclusions

Societies confronted by global ecological risks have to face the unknown (Beck, 1999). The post–World War II faith in unlimited economic growth is weakening because of the danger of growing environmental degradation. In a world of such incertitude, many people may fear change and search for security in dogma or apocalyptic discourse, but we may also find a unique opportunity to create equitable, sustainable learning communities and to make lifelong learning a reality for all.

The educational process can no longer confine its activities to transmitting culturally determined knowledge required to precede entry into a stable adult world that will supposedly remain relevant throughout life.

Environmental lifelong education is, and will by necessity increasingly become more so, a process focused on the empowerment of people and communities in relationship to a changing environment. Lifelong environmental education is summoned to become more and more relevant to the challenge of being more life-rooted, life-oriented, and life-wide. Educators cannot ignore the ecological dimension of learning that enhances learning's active and creative character, and therefore its ecological sustainability. Sustainability cannot occur without active citizenship that itself requires sustainable environmental learning.

References

Abrahamsson, K. *The Expanding Learning Enterprise in Sweden*. Paris: OECD, 1990.

Ardoino, J., and Lourau, R. *Les Pédagogies Institutionnelles*. Paris: PUF, 1994.

Beck, U. *World Risk Society*. Cambridge, Mass.: Blackwell, 1999.

Beck, U., Giddens, A., and Lash, S. *Reflexive Modernization*. Cambridge, Mass.: Polity Press, 1994.

Bélanger, P. "Lifelong Learning: The Dynamics of Lifelong Educations." In P. Bélanger and E. Gelpi (eds.), *Lifelong Education*. Hamburg: IRE Library, 1995.

Bélanger, P., and Tuijnman, A. *New Patterns of Adult Learning: A Six-Country Comparative Study*. Oxford: Pergamon and Unesco Institute for Education, 1997.

Bronfenbrenner, U., and Morris, P. A. "The Ecology of Developmental Processes." In R. M. Lerner (ed.), *Handbook of Child Psychology*. Vol. 1: *Theory*. (5th ed.) New York: Wiley, 1997.

Chadwick, A., and Stannett, A. *European Perspectives on Museums and the Education of Adults*. Leicester, England: National Institute of Adult Continuing Education, 1998.

Cohen, M. D., and Sproull, L. S. (eds.). *Organizational Learning*. Thousand Oaks, Calif.: Sage, 1995.

Collins, A., Greeno, J. G., and Resnick, L. B. "Environments for Learning." In A. Tuijnman (ed.), *International Encyclopedia of Adult Education and Training*. Oxford, England: Pergamon, 1996.

Delors, J. "Learning: The Treasure Within." *Report to UNESCO of the International Commission on Education for the Twenty-First Century*. Paris: UNESCO, 1996.

Dumond, R. *Ouvrez les Yeux* [Open Your Eyes]. Paris: Arléa, 2000.

Frischkopf, A. (ed.). *Weiterbildung und Museums* [Lifelong Education and Museums]. Soest, Germany: Landesinstitut für Schule und Weiterbildung, 1994.

Gibson, J. *The Ecological Approach to Visual Perception*. Boston: Houghton Mifflin, 1979.

Harman, W., and Porter, M. *The New Business of Business: Sharing Responsibilities for a Positive Global Future*. San Francisco: Berrett-Koehler, 1997.

Harvey, D. *The Condition of Postmodernity*. Oxford, England: Blackwell, 1990.

Hautecoeur, J. P. *Éducation Écologique dans la Vie Quotidienne* [Ecological Education in Daily Life]. Quebec: Ministère de l'Education, 2000.

Lave, J., and Wenger, E. *Situated Learning: Legitimate Peripheral Participation*. Cambridge, England: Cambridge University Press, 1991.

Lewicki, J. *Cooperative Ecology and Place: Development of a Pedagogy of Place Curriculum*. Wis.: Kickapoo River Institute, 1997.

McIlroy, J., and Westwood, S. *Border Country: Raymond Williams in Adult Education*. Leicester, England: National Institute of Adult Continuing Education, 1993.

Olson, D. "Review of *Toward a Literate Society*." *Proceedings of the National Academy of Education*. New York: McGraw-Hill, 1975.

Orefice, P. *Politiche e Interventi Culturali e Formativi in Italia Nel Secondo Novecento* [Politics and Culture in Italy in the Second Half of the Twentieth Century]. Naples, Italy: Ferraro, 1991.

Orellana, I. *La Communauté d'Apprentissage en Éducation Relative à l'Environnement: Signification, Dynamiques et Enjeux* [Community Training in Environmental Education: Stakeholders, Action, Significance]. Unpublished doctoral dissertation, University of Quebec in Montreal, 2002.

O'Sullivan, E. *Transformative Learning: Education Vision for the 21st Century.* London: Zed Books, 1999.

Robottom, I., and Hart, P. *Research in Environmental Education.* Victoria, Australia: Deakin University Press, 1993.

Rothwell, W. J., and Kazanas, H. C. *Human Resource Development: A Strategic Approach.* Amherst, Mass.: Human Resource Development Press, 1994.

Sauvé, L. "Recherche et Formation en Éducation Relative à l'Environnement: Une Dynamique Réflexive [Research and Training in Environmental Education: Reflective Action]." *Éducation Permanente,* 2001, *148,* 2,001–2,003.

Schön, D. *The Reflective Practitioner: How Professionals Think in Action.* New York: Basic Books, 1983.

Senge, P. M. *The Fifth Discipline: The Art and Practice of the Learning Organization.* New York: Doubleday, 1990.

Sterling, S. *Sustainable Education: Re-Visioning Learning and Change.* Schumacher Briefings, no. 6. Bristol, England: Schumacher Briefings, 2001.

UNESCO. *Report of the Fifth International Conference on Adult Education.* Paris: UNESCO, 1997.

UNICEF and Inter-Agency Commission. *World Declaration on Education for All and Framework for Action to Meet Basic Learning Needs.* New York: UNICEF, 1990.

Wagner, S. *Alphabétisme et Alphabétisation au Canada* [The Elimination of Illiteracy in Canada]. Ottawa: Commission Canadienne pour l'UNESCO, 2002.

Watkins, K. E. "Workplace Learning: Changing Times, Changing Practices." In W. F. Spikes (ed.), *Workplace Learning.* New Directions for Adult and Continuing Education, no. 68. San Francisco: Jossey-Bass, 1995.

Watkins, K. E., and Marsick, V. J. *Sculpting the Learning Organizations: Lessons in the Art and Science of Change.* San Francisco: Jossey-Bass, 1993.

Wenger, E. *Communities of Practice: Learning, Meaning, and Identity.* Cambridge, England: Cambridge University Press, 1998.

Whalen, J. "Conversation Analysis." In E. F. Borgatta and M. L. Borgatta (eds.), *The Encyclopedia of Sociology.* New York: Macmillan, 1992.

World Commission on Environment and Development. *Our Common Future* [the Brundtland Report]. Oxford: Oxford University Press, 1987.

Ziaka, Y., Robichon, P., and others. *Éducation et L'Environnement: Six Propositions pour Agir Entre Citoyens* [Education and the Environment: Six Propositions for Citizen Action]. New York: McGraw-Hill, 2002.

PAUL BÉLANGER, *a former director of UNESCO, is professor and director of the Interdisciplinary Research and Development Centre on Lifelong Learning (CIRDEP) at the University of Quebec in Montreal.*

9

This final chapter summarizes the important themes of environmental adult education as they are conceptualized in this volume, and provides suggestions for further reading.

Learning Patterns of Landscape and Life

Darlene E. Clover, Lilian H. Hill

In this chapter, we explore some of the key themes that emerged from this volume and offer suggestions for future reading. We believe that environmental problems are situated on a personal-political continuum. They are personal because they are felt at individual, family, and community levels, and for many, constitute a struggle for existence and identity. They are political because they arise from the ideological frameworks and economic development strategies of capitalist globalization.

Ecological deterioration will soon eclipse ideological conflict as the dominant national security concern throughout the world. The aggressive demand for natural resources means that wars and civic struggle will continue to rise. Beginning in the 1980s, studies began to show that already, more than half of the world's population was living in cities, links were becoming more apparent between air pollution and respiratory diseases, and "morbidity in terms of cancer, bronchitis, and emphysema" was on the rise (Douglas, 1983, p. 167). For adult education to be effective in dealing with the contemporary environmental crisis, its theories and methodologies must be rethought and re-created. This does not mean simply adding environmental issues and stirring, but rather entering into new spheres of knowledge, spirit, practice, and political action.

A time of crisis exists "when the old is dead but the new is not yet born" (Bandarage, 1997, p. 3). It is, to the Chinese, a time of both "danger" and "opportunity." While no one expects education to deal with the environmental crisis single-handedly, expectations and anxieties have raised the level of demand for new approaches to teaching and learning (Smyth, 1995). The fundamental challenge for environmental adult educators world-

New Directions for Adult and Continuing Education, no. 99, Fall 2003 © Wiley Periodicals, Inc.

wide has been to articulate a theory and practice that adequately addresses contemporary social and environmental problems, encapsulates the complexity of human-earth relations, and provides new ways of learning to live with the earth on just and equitable terms. Collectively, the authors in this sourcebook rise to the challenge by developing new ecologically based teaching and learning frameworks. These approaches respect and nurture patterns of knowing that are rooted in the spirit and the land; they provide opportunities to critique, reflect, and experience; they challenge language structure or governance; and they encourage hope, imagination, creativity, and action.

Spirit and Landscape of Knowledge

Knowing is contextual and relational. It is an ongoing, creative, and dynamic act that is fundamental to the process of living. Environmental adult education does not abstract knowledge from the knower, nor the context from the lived process of knowing. Clover (Chapter One) and Kapoor (Chapter Five) recognize the depth, breadth, and relationship to the land of many indigenous peoples and women who continue to live more subsistence-based lifestyles. These knowledges, which highlight human-planet connections and inform song, dance, history, and ritual, can make a substantial contribution to our understanding of a pedagogy of respect for the land and an ecological epistemology. In spite of increased disconnections between humans and the rest of nature brought on by contemporary discourses and practices described by L. H. Hill and Johnston in Chapter Two, Sumner (Chapter Four) and Karlovic and Patrick (Chapter Six) uncover understandings of the need for a rich and healthy natural environment that many Western women and rural communities retain.

However, all of these authors recognize that we are engaged in a process of denying recognition of the ecological knowledge of most of the world's people. The marginalization and destruction of environmental knowledge(s) are of primary concern to environmental adult education because this lived process of knowing has extraordinary ramifications for the survival of people and cultures.

Critical, Spiritual, and Experiential Frameworks of Learning

Bélanger in Chapter Eight suggests that, for the most part, what exists as adult environmental or public education is simply the transmission of environmental data or facts from "expert" to "nonexpert." He believes that we need to challenge learning environments that reinforce antienvironmental messages. St. Clair (Chapter Seven) supports this by challenging high levels of "Western" scientific knowledge as the only basis for environmental adult literacy, and exploring how this framework becomes a recipe for elitism. Transmission as a form of education neither respects nor engages the adult learner but rather dichotomizes knowledge and knowers and depoliticizes learning by assigning individual blame.

Kapoor (Chapter Five) and Karlovic and Patrick (Chapter Six) outline pedagogical strategies that engage learners and tap into their existing "ecological" knowledge(s) and experiences—whether they be cognitive, emotional, or spiritual ways of knowing. By using this practice, they develop a critical consciousness of the root causes of environmental problems, uncover complexities such as complicity, and often help to promote more informed and strategic political activism.

L. H. Hill and Johnston (Chapter Two) and Sumner (Chapter Four) articulate ideas of contextualized learning. Environmental adult education should use outdoor learning for the dual purposes of provoking outrage and encouraging awe, wonder, and a renewed faith in human capacity to create change. By learning in place, we begin to see the community and its surrounding environment as a landscape of resistance, a source of regeneration, and a site of inspiration, beauty, or neglect. This can help to bring people back in touch with their emotional, spiritual, and psychological connections to the land and thereby widen a sense of self and community.

Capitalist Globalization and Environmental Oppressions

Clover (Chapter One), R. J. Hill (Chapter Three), Sumner (Chapter Four), and Kapoor (Chapter Five) all challenge us to recognize the profound cultural and ecological implications of economic development and corporate globalization. While the scientific and industrial revolutions created environmental upheavals, contemporary capitalist globalization has even greater ability to destroy. These authors remind us that maintaining democracy cannot be done from the top down, but must come from within urban and rural communities. However, environmental adult education must also question relations of power—in particular, gendered and race relations—in society. Communities are not monolithic, and in their confines, women, indigenous peoples, and people of color are often more vulnerable to the impact of globalization and environmental deterioration but have the least resources and opportunities to fight back. Within the discourse of power, L. H. Hill and Johnston remind us in Chapter Two that the rest of nature is also a victim of oppression, and this fact must guide our educational work around justice and equity.

Clover (Chapter One), Karlovic and Patrick (Chapter Six), and St. Clair (Chapter Seven) address a key basis of globalization—consumption and production. But rather than blaming individuals, and particularly women, for lifestyle choices, Clover constructs a critical media framework and analyzes marketing practices that perpetuate the "good life" based on material ownership and conceal practices of overproduction and unethical resource extraction. Karlovic and Patrick comment on the unconscious nature of complicity and provide an example of how this can be raised and discussed openly through a collective learning process.

In Chapter Two, L. H. Hill and Johnston raise the point that humans have more than simply a material relationship with the rest of nature, they also have a spiritual bond with and in nature. The impact of development and capitalist globalization has, for many, broken this bond and created a profound sense of emptiness, loneliness, and loss. Environmental adult education legitimizes and valorizes concerns for spirituality and the environment in order to both heal and grow.

Ecological Language and Literacy

L. H. Hill and Johnston (Chapter Two) demonstrate that language is neither neutral nor value-free but rather constitutes a site of ideological struggle. Their analysis elucidates the unconscious hierarchies of power relations and violence against the rest of nature that are embedded within our linguistic practices. They call for new metaphors that can better help us to understand ourselves and our relationships to the rest of nature. The women participating in Karlovic and Patrick's (Chapter Six) environmental adult education workshop call for a language of interconnectedness that can become as commonplace as that of the terminology associated with the military and other forces of violence and dominance. Patterns of communication in environmental adult education need to move beyond unintentionally perpetuating domination and help us to find a "quietness of mind" that allows empathy, sharing, and collaboration.

St. Clair (Chapter Seven) examines language through the lens of adult literacy and examines constructed meanings in text and signs. He argues for an ecological literacy that can address the missing element of critical engagement. From an adult education framework, he challenges the decision-making tenets of environmental education that is immersed in individualism and monetary costs, and he draws attention to the larger implications for health and well-being.

Activism and Environmental Adult Education

In the warp of problems and critique lies the weave of hope. R. J. Hill (Chapter Three), Clover (Chapter One), and Kapoor (Chapter Five) provide numerous examples of powerful partnerships between adult education and activism. Farm workers in California organize and educate against poisoning pesticides; women in Nigeria organize sit-ins and challenge the oil industry to be responsible to the community; aboriginal peoples in India challenge the inadequacy of government development programs geared toward economics; and antiglobalization protesters worldwide organize teach-ins that focus on understanding complex United Nations structures.

Meanwhile, women in Canada develop critical aesthetic learning opportunities to challenge development, university-based adult educators in New Zealand encourage experiential ecological learning to transform the university, First Nations educators introduce and legitimize practices of resistance and defiance as tools of learning, and elderly people in the United States put forward counternarratives to war and violence. These courageous and imaginative acts not only give us hope, but signal ways forward.

Clover (Chapter One), Sumner (Chapter Four), and Bélanger (Chapter Eight) argue that another important way forward is to build new partnerships or even become activists ourselves. The local, global, and political nature of environmental problems requires that we make links to community-based and sometimes multilevel political action. For environmental adult educators, this means we can become aligned with contemporary ideas and practices and in turn assist these groups to strengthen their educational capacities by building networks of working conversations based on critical reflection, debate, laughter, and hope.

But St. Clair reminds us in Chapter Seven that although taking direct action is an important component of environmental adult education, it should not be seen as the only valuable outcome. There must be respect for learning in and of itself and for the fact that some people will never use their knowledge and learning to become activists. It is also important to recognize that different dimensions of action exist. Taking action does not always have to be "doing something" in the manual sense. An action may be making a decision, revising a particular point of view, posing a new problem or question, or reframing a structure of meaning. Knowledge that lends itself to use should not be seen as superior to that which is contemplative.

Future Reading

Environmental adult education is a new stream of adult education and is still very much a work in progress. This means that unlike other areas of adult education, materials on this topic are somewhat limited. Nevertheless, they do exist and are growing in numbers. This volume addresses a number of issues and concerns raised in environmental adult education and highlights numerous practices. For those who wish to delve more deeply into the discourse of the field, the references at the conclusion of each chapter provide an excellent beginning. In this final chapter, we provide a brief annotated bibliography of references the reader may wish to seek out.

Clover, D. E. *Global Perspectives in Environmental Adult Education: Justice, Sustainability, and Transformation.* New York: Peter Lang, 2003.
    This book emerges from the work of the global Learning for Environmental Action Programme (LEAP). The twelve chapters are grouped together under the concepts of ecological knowledge, feminist learning and activism, and practice and research methods. Writing from platforms of

community or the academy, the authors from Australia, Canada, Fiji, India, Kenya, Mexico, the Philippines, Sudan, and the United States enrich epistemological debates, provide new theoretical frameworks, and create new human-earth pedagogical practices of critique and creativity.

Clover, D. E., Follen, S., and Hall, B. L. *The Nature of Transformation: Environmental Adult Education*. (2nd ed.) Toronto: University of Toronto Press, 2000.

This text provides fifty pages of hands-on practical activities that stimulate critical thinking and creativity, use nature as a teacher and site of learning, and weave together environmental, cultural, economic, political, and social issues. Because environmental issues are so vast and complex, activities demonstrate how to deal with issues ranging from soil erosion to healthy food, from consumerism to gender oppression, and from corporatization to environmental racism. There are also ideas for organizing workshops within an ecological context; examples of activities from Australia, the Philippines, Fiji, and Hong Kong; and a list of feminist, adult, and environmental adult education resources and organizations. This text can be purchased by contacting the author at clover@uvic.ca.

International Council for Adult Education (ICAE). *Convergence*. Toronto: ICAE.

Convergence is a global quarterly journal of adult education that addresses issues, practices, and developments in the broad field of adult and nonformal education. Two thematic issues of *Convergence* focus on environmental adult education (copies can be purchased by contacting clover@uvic.ca):

1. *Volume 33, Number 3, 2000*
   Articles in this edition examine arts and creativity as learning and mobilizing tools of environmental adult education and focus on diverse aspects of environmental popular education in India and Mexico. One area of particular importance to adult learning that is raised in a number of articles is the impact of women's ecological knowledge on socioenvironmental change. Other authors explore the needs—and the strengths and weaknesses—of education and training for environmental organizations in Australia and communities in the Philippines and the Caribbean.
2. *Volume 28, Number 4, 1995*
   In this edition, various authors describe the challenges of using popular theater as a tool of environmental adult education in Canada and the Philippines and debate the merits of sustainable development as a framework for learning and change. Other articles describe university-based experiential learning practices and examine theoretical foundations and frameworks of environmental adult education in Canadian

and Chilean contexts. In South Africa, women take on government-sanctioned environmental racism while in Fiji they use nature as a teacher and site of learning to challenge development. Authors from Europe and Africa focus on the role of the media as a tool of nonformal ecological learning.

Leal Filho, W. (ed.). *Lifelong Learning and Environmental Education.* Frankfurt: Peter Lang, 1997.

This book contains chapters from around the world that deal with environmental issues within the contexts of adult education, community-based education, and quality of learning. Authors from Canada, Italy, Germany, Poland, Slovakia, and Pakistan challenge pedagogical practices of information transmission and argue for more interactive approaches and communication strategies that provide people with opportunities to participate and take appropriate actions to improve the quality of their lives and environments.

O'Sullivan, E. *Transformative Learning: Educational Vision for the 21st Century.* Toronto: University of Toronto Press, 1999.

O'Sullivan proposes an ecozoic vision for education to heal the self-imposed divisions between humans and the earth and guide us in the struggle for planetary survival and sustainability. Transformative learning requires a holistic, integrative approach based in generative principles of unity, participation and integration that support social justice, peace, and sustainability. Contemporary goals of education are to repudiate the dysfunctional values of the global marketplace, foster human connection with place, encourage diversity, and further more responsible human participation in an extended global community.

References

Bandarage, A. *Women, Population, and Global Crisis: A Political-Economic Analysis.* London: Zed Books, 1997.

Douglas, I. *The Urban Environment.* London: Edward Arnold, 1983.

Smyth, J. "Environment and Education: A View of a Changing Scene." *Environmental Education Research,* 1995, *1*(1), 3–20.

DARLENE E. CLOVER *is assistant professor of adult education in the Faculty of Education, University of Victoria, British Columbia.*

LILIAN H. HILL *is education specialist and assistant professor at Virginia Commonwealth University in Richmond, Virginia.*

INDEX

Abrahamsson, K., 84, 87

Activism: barriers to, 1; environmental adult educators and, 12–13, 73–74, 75, 92–93; environmental literacy and, 69–77; environmental popular education and, 47–55, 73–74; importance of environmental education for, 73–74; participatory research and, 33. *See also* Social change; Social movement learning; Social movements and protests

Adivasis, 47–55

Adult education. *See* Environmental adult education

Africa: ecological and antiglobalization movements in, 7, 12, 85–86, 92; environmental issues of, 20

Agency, conscious human, 42

Agenda 21, 27, 83

Agriculture: environmental justice and, 29; indigenous knowledge of, 54–55

Allen, D. W., 32, 37

Allen, P. L., 40, 45

Anderson, Y. B., 27, 37

Anti-environmental education, 32

Antiglobalization movements, 7, 12–13, 33–34, 85–86, 92–93

Antiwar movement, 12, 31

Appadurai, A., 6, 11, 14

Appiko movement, 50

Ardoino, J., 81, 87

Asia Watch, 50, 55

Associated Press, 59

Asun, J. M., 30, 33, 36

Athman, J. A., 71, 77

Attention, 63–64, 65, 67

Autokoenomy, 64, 67

Ayres, R., 40

Bacon, F., 74

Bandarage, A., 89, 95

Bandyopadhyay, J., 50, 56

Barndt, D., 47, 53, 56

Barton, D., 77

Bateson, M. C., 20, 25, 63, 68

Baviskar, A., 49, 50, 56

Bean, W. E., 24, 25

Beck, U., 82, 86, 87

Bélanger, P., 3, 79, 80, 87, 88, 90, 93

Bellamy Foster, J., 6, 14

Benton, T., 43, 45

Berreman, G., 50, 56

Bharat Aluminum Company (BALCO), 50

Boal, B., 51, 57

Boerner, C., 32, 36

Boggs, C., 51, 53, 56

Botswana, 20

Bowers, C. A., 20, 25

Brazil, environmentalism in, 7

Brecher, J., 40, 45

Bronfenbrenner, U., 80, 87

Brundtland Report, 79

Bullard, R. D., 28, 29, 36

Bush, G., 12

Byrne, J., 6, 14

Camacho, D. E., 31, 35, 36, 37

Canada: democracy in, 13; environmental adult education in, 1, 11, 12, 93

Capitalism, globalization and, 6–10, 33, 42, 91–92. *See also* Corporatization; Globalization

Capra, F., 18, 22, 25

Carmona, E., 11, 14

Carroll, W., 51, 56

Carter, R. E., 21, 25

Center for Health, Environment, and Justice (CHEJ), 75–77

Center for the Study of American Business, 32

Chadwick, A., 82, 87

Chakravarty, K., 48, 56

Chawla, L., 73–74, 77

Chicano organizing, 27

Chipko peasant movement, 50

Chowdhary, K., 49, 56

Christ, C. O., 22, 26

Citizen's Clearinghouse for Hazardous Waste, 75

Civil commons, 42–43, 44, 45

Civil society, 1

Clarke, T., 9, 11, 13, 14

Clover, D. E., 1–2, 3, 5, 7, 8, 9, 10, 11, 12, 14, 15, 21, 25, 33, 36, 47, 56, 89, 90, 91–94, 95

Cognitive development, ecology of, 80

Cohen, M. D., 80, 87

Cole, P., 6, 14

Colleges, environmental adult education in, 11
Collins, A., 84, 87
Communities: environmental adult education in, 11–12, 13, 85; experience of self in, 64; low-income, public participation by, 35
Communities of practices, 85–86
Community-driven environmental justice education and research, 32–33
Community sustainability, 2, 19, 39–45; challenges to, 39–41; civil commons and, 42–43, 44, 45; environmental adult education and, 39–45; environmental learning and, 43–44; environmental lifelong learning and, 86–87; framework for, 41–44; globalization and, 2, 39–45, 91–92
Conn, S. A., 20, 22, 25
Consumerism, 7–8; environmental adult education about, 11; environmental sexism and racism and, 9–10, 31–32; externalization of, 42; lifestyle choices and pressures of, 59–60, 91–92
Convergence (ICAE), 94–95
Coppola, N., 71, 77
Corporatization, 8–9, 13, 33, 63; community sustainability and, 39–46. See also Globalization
Costello, T., 40, 45
Cox, R., 51, 56
Cranton, P., 61, 66, 68
Crisis, 89–90
Critical social-structural reflection, 52–53
Cronon, W., 18, 25
Cultural learning environments, 82
Cultural metaphors, 19–21
Cultural politics of science, 32–33, 53–54
Cunningham, P. M., 30, 36
Cuomo, C. J., 9, 14, 19, 25

Daloz, L. A., 23, 25
Daly, H. E., 40, 45
Dam-related movements, in India, 50
Danielson, L. E., 36
Darni stones, 52–53
De-Shalit, A., 35, 36
Death, globalization and, 6–7, 9
Deep ecology, 18, 19
Deforestation, in India, 48–49, 50, 54–55
Dei, G., 54, 56
Delors, J., 80, 87

Democracy, 1, 2; environmental, 30, 31–32, 35; globalization and threats to, 13, 42–43; popular education and, 47–48
Dendinger, R., 72, 77
Desai, N., 50, 56
Dewey, J., 30
Dhanagre, D. N., 49, 56
Di Chiro, G., 18, 25
Dirkx, J. M., 23, 25
Disinger, J. F., 70, 77
Distributive justice, 28, 34
Diversity, 74–75
D'Monte, D., 50, 56
Dopp, S., 11, 14
Doran, D., 12
Douglas, I., 89, 95
Dualism, 18–19; language and, 19–21
Dumond, R., 81, 87
Duval, J., 8, 14
Duyker, E., 49, 56

Earth Day, 34, 61
Earth Summit, 27, 79, 83
East Asian tiger economies, 40
Ecojustice, 28
Ecological base, 24
Ecological feminism, 18–19, 74
Ecological identity, 19
Ecological justice, 28
Ecological learning, 80–81, 85
Ecological lens, 14
Ecological philosophies, 18–19
Ecology of cognitive development, 80
Ecology of learning, 3, 79–87
Economic discourse, 31–32
Ecozoic consciousness, 21, 95
Educational management organizations (EMOs), 41
Eisenberg, E., 20, 25
Ellwood, W., 40, 45
Emotional links, in language, 21–22
Endangered Species Act, 42
English, L. M., 23, 25
Environment and Development in the USA, 33, 36
Environmental Activists Share Knowledge and Experiences, 33, 36
Environmental adult education (EAE): challenges to, from market sector power, 41, 83, 84; community sustainability and, 39–45; as critical lens, 14, 73; definitions and features of, 10–11; ecology of learning and,

79–87; economic discourse in, 31–32, 41; environmental justice and, 27–36; environmental literacy and, 69–77; environmental organizations and, 13; globalization and, 1–2, 5–14, 33–34, 41, 91–92; humanity's relationship to nature and, 17–25; importance of, 1, 3, 73–75; initiatives of, 85–86; language and metaphor in, 17–25, 92; learning environments and, 79–87; about lifestyle choices, 60–67; linkages with, 1–2, 10–14, 24, 27–36, 79, 89–95; nature and, 24–25; overview and themes of, 1–3, 89–95; practices of, 11–12; readings on, 93–95; reconceptualization of, 43–44; social movement learning and, 2, 11, 30–31, 34–36, 47–55, 59–67, 75–77, 92–93; spirituality in, 22–23, 92; task of, 17–18, 89–90; for women, 59–67

Environmental adult educators: activism and, 12–13, 73–74, 92–93; task of, 89–90

Environmental Education Plan, 85

Environmental equity, 28

Environmental issues: crisis of, 89–90; environmental adult education linkages with, 1–2, 10–14, 24, 27–36, 79, 89–95; of globalization, 6–10, 20–21, 40; importance of, in adult education context, 1

Environmental justice (EJ), 2, 27–36; activities and concerns of, 28–29; adult education and learning in, 2, 30–36; community-driven education and research in, 32–33; defined, 27, 28–29; economic discourse and, 31–32; globalization and, 33–34; movement of, 27–28; names for, 28; popular education in, 29, 30, 33–36

Environmental lifelong learning (ELL), 79–87; book about, 95; concepts of, 83–84; ecological perspectives on that challenge the formal education system, 84–85; non-ecological lifelong learning *versus*, 84; principles of, 85

Environmental literacy, 3, 69–77; action and, 69–77; attributes of, 71–73; creating critical, 69–77; definitions of, 70; examples of, 75–77; roots of, 69–71; shaping adult education for, 73–75

Environmental organizations, environmental adult education and, 13

Environmental philosophies, 18–19

Environmental popular education (EPE), 2, 47–55; environmental justice and, 29, 30, 33–36; about globalization, 33–34; in indigenous social movements of India, 47–55; practical considerations of, 50–51; prefigurative role for, 51; theoretical considerations of, 50–51; for women, 59–67. *See also* Social movement learning

Environmental public education interventions, 83–84

Environmental sustainability, 19. *See also* Community sustainability; Sustainability

Ethnicity, 1

Experience, 3, 80, 84

Falk, I., 43, 45

Families, globalization and, 9–10

Farm worker campaigns, 27, 92

Feminist ecology, 18–19, 74

Feminist environmental adult education, 12

Feminist environmental philosophy, 19

Feminist movement, language of, 21

Fernandes, W., 49, 56

Films, 65, 67

Finger, M., 30, 33, 36, 41, 45

First Nations educators, 12

Foley, G., 41, 45

Follen, S., 9, 14, 21, 25, 47, 56, 94

Follett, M. P., 62, 68

Footprints International, 11

Foucault, M., 34, 36

Fractured worldviews, 20–21, 22, 92

Freire, P., 47, 53, 56, 73, 74, 77

Frischkopf, A., 82, 87

Gadgil, M., 48, 56

Gandhamadan Adivasi movement, 50

Gandhi, M., 48

Gibbs, L., 75–76

Gibson, J., 80, 87

Giddens, A., 82, 87

Gillen, M. A., 25

Global climate justice movement, 28

Global Perspectives in Environmental Adult Education (Clover), 93–94

"Globalism Project," 40, 45

Globalization, 3, 5–14; community sustainability and, 2, 39–45; definitions of, 6, 33; environmental adult education and, 1–2, 5–14, 33–34; environmental justice and popular education

about, 33–36, 91–92; institutions of, 33; language and metaphor of, 20–21, 92; socioenvironmental impacts of, 5–10, 13–14, 20–21, 33, 39–41
Glover, L., 6, 14
Goldsmith, E., 40, 45
Gottlieb, R., 35, 36
Gramsci, A., 51, 56
Grandinetti, L., 11, 14
Grassroots movement learning, 30–31, 34–36; for confronting knowledge experts, 32–33; examples of, 75–77
Green consumerism, 10
Green Party, 30, 62
Greenbelt Movement, 7
Greene, M., 11, 14
Greeno, J. G., 84, 87
Greenpeace, 59
Griffiths, J., 8, 14
Growth imperative, 40
Guevara, J. R., 29, 36
Guha, R., 48, 56

Habermas, J., 30, 36
Hall, B. L., 9, 14, 21, 25, 47, 56, 94
Hamilton, M., 77
Harman, W., 84, 87
Harris, E., 6, 9, 13, 14
Hart, M., 30, 36
Hart, P., 83, 88
Harvey, D., 51, 56, 82, 87
Hautecoeur, J. P., 79, 87
Health: globalization and, 9–10; spirituality and, 22–23
Heaney, T., 30, 36
Hegde, P., 50, 56
Hegemony, 2, 51
Herstory, 67
Highlander Education and Research Center, 33
Hill, K. M., 32, 37
Hill, L. H., 2, 3, 17, 26, 89, 90, 91, 92, 95
Hill, R. J., 2, 27, 30, 32, 37, 38, 91, 92
Hoagland, S. L., 63, 64, 68
Hopelessness, 1
Horseman, 7
Horton, M., 73, 75, 77
Hynes, N. P., 35, 37

Ibikunle-Johnson, V., 31, 37
Illinois Department of Natural Resources, 71, 77
Imagination, 11

India: Adivasis in, 47–55; environmental popular education in, 2, 47–55; indigenous social movements in, 2, 47–55; Jharkhand region of, 50; Orissa, 48, 50, 51; postindependence development in, 48–50, 51
Indigenous peoples: environmental justice (EJ) movement and, 27, 29, 34, 76–77; environmental literacy for, 76–77; environmental popular education with, 2, 29, 34, 47–55; environmental racism and, 10; knowledge of, 52–55, 90; social movements of, in India, 47–55, 92
Information-education-communication (IEC) strategy, 83–84
Institutional pedagogies, 81
Inter-Agency Commission, 83, 88
Interdependence/interconnection: community sustainability and, 42–43; dualistic worldview versus, 20–21; ecological philosophies and, 18–19, 74; environmental adult education about, 17–19, 21–22, 24–25; environmental justice and, 34–35; environmental popular education and, 52–55; indigenous cosmology and, 52–53; spirituality and, 22–23, 92
International Adult Literacy Survey, 70, 77
International Council for Adult Education (ICAE), 94–95
International Day Against Consumption, 34
International Forum, 85
International Monetary Fund (IMF), 33, 83
International Work Group for Indigenous Affairs (IWGIA), 49, 56–57
International Workers Day, 34
Iraq, 7
Italy, laboratory for education in, 81–82
Ivanic, R., 77

Jansen, L., 13, 14
Johnson, M., 20, 26
Johnston, J. D., 2, 17, 26, 90, 91, 92
Journal of Educational Sociology, 61
Jubilee Movement International, 34

K-12 environmental education, 83
Kapoor, D., 2, 29, 30, 37, 47, 51, 53, 57, 90, 91, 92

Karlovic, L., 2, 59, 68, 90, 91–92
Karpiak, I. E., 22, 25
Kazanas, H. C., 80, 88
Keen, C. H., 23, 25
Keen, J. P., 23, 25
Keough, N., 11, 14
Kilpatrick, S., 43, 45
King, A., 32, 37
Knowledge: environmental literacy and, 69–77; Kondh cosmological, 52–53; Kondh ecological, 53–55; landscape of, 90; power and, 47, 52–55; transmission of, 90–91
Knowledge experts, 32–33
Kohl, H., 77
Kohl, J., 77
Kohli, A., 48, 57
Kondh Adivasis, 47–55
Kothari, R., 49, 57
Kothari, S., 49, 57
Kovan, J. T., 23, 25
Krall, F. R., 60, 61, 64, 68
Kui songs, 52–53
Kyoto Agreement, 42

LaChapelle, D., 62, 68
Lahaye, M., 8, 15
Lake, D. C., 21, 25
Lakoff, G., 20, 26
Lambert, T., 32, 36
Landless Rural Workers Movement, 7
Landscape of knowledge, 90
Language: in adult education classrooms, 21–22, 24–25; concepts of nature reflected in, 2, 17–25, 92; ecological, 79–87; emotional links in, 21–22
Lash, S., 82, 87
Lave, J., 82, 87
Leal Filho, W., 95
Learning, 43–44; critical frameworks of, 90–91; ecology of, 3, 79–87; environment lifelong, 79–87; experiential frameworks of, 90–91; spiritual frameworks of, 90–91, 92
Learning environments, 79–87; concepts of, 80–83; environmental lifelong learning in, 83–87
Learning for Environmental Action Programme (LEAP), 93–94
Learning organization, 80
Learning society, 80
Lee, K. N., 45
Lengwati, D. M., 10, 15, 29, 37

Lester, J. P., 32, 37
Lewicki, J., 81, 87
Life values, 42, 44
Lifelong learning, non-ecological, 84. *See also* Environmental lifelong learning
Lifelong Learning and Environmental Education (Leal Filho), 95
Lifestyle choices, 60–67, 91–92
Lindeman, E. C., 30, 61, 66
Lindqvist, S., 81
Literacy, 3, 69, 70, 71–72, 77, 80. *See also* Environmental literacy
Literate environment, 80
Local-based environmental adult education, 44–45, 74
Loneliness, 22
Los Coyotes, 76–77
Lourau, R., 81, 87
Love Canal, 75–76
Lowy, M., 7, 15
Loyalist College, Ontario, 11

Maathai, W., 7
Mack, J. E., 20, 26
Mager, R. F., 73, 77
Mandela, N., 7
Market sector power, 32, 83
Marketing: of adult education, 41; globalization and, 8, 13, 20–21, 41; with natural symbols, 81
Marsick, V. J., 80, 88
Marx, K., 6
Mayo, P., 6, 13, 15, 47, 51, 53, 54, 57
McIlroy, J., 81, 87
McKenzie, L., 20, 26
McKeown-Ice, R., 72, 77
McMurtry, J., 42–43, 45
Media information, 59, 81, 84
Melucci, A., 51, 57
Merchant, C., 19, 26
Meriah, 52–53
Merrifield, J., 32, 35, 37
Metaphor: in adult education classrooms, 21–22, 24–25; concepts of nature reflected in, 2, 17–18, 19–21; cultural, 19–21; of literacy, 77; military or violent, 17, 22, 92
Mies, M., 9, 15, 74, 77
Miller, G. T., 30, 31, 37
Miller, K., 12, 15
Miller, R., 24, 26
Mische, P. M., 44, 45
Monkman, K., 6, 15, 33, 37

Monroe, M. C., 71, 77
Moore, T., 22–23, 26
Morris, P. A., 87
Morrison, R., 30, 31, 37
Multi-Purpose Training and Employment Association, 12
Mythology, Kondh, 52–53

Nandy, A., 49, 51, 57
Narmada River Valley Project, 49, 50
Nash, K., 31, 37
National Institute of Adult Continuing Education, 73, 77
National origin, 1
National People of Color Environmental Leadership Summits, 27, 28
Natural resources: environmental justice and, 34–36; globalization and, 6–7, 9–10, 20–21, 42
Natural world: environmental adult education and, 24–25; environmental justice and, 34; humanity's relationship with, 2, 17–25, 74; language and metaphor about, 2, 17–25, 92
Nature of Transformation, The (Clover, Follen, Hall), 94
Nayak, R., 51, 57
"Needle and thread" protest, 11–12
Nehru, J., 48
Newman, M., 30, 34, 37, 75
Newman, P., 77
Nigeria, social and environmental movements in, 7, 12, 92
Nongovernmental organizations, environmental adult education by, 11–12, 33–34
Novotny, P., 27, 31, 36, 37
NO$_x$ emissions, 72

Oliver, B., 29, 37
Olson, D., 80, 87
Omvedt, G., 49, 57
Oommen, T. K., 49, 57
Oppression, 1, 2, 3; environmental justice and, 27–36; environmental popular education and, 47–55; environmental problems and, 24; globalization and, 6–7, 91–92; of indigenous peoples of India, 47–55; language and, 20–22, 23, 24. See also Social injustice
Orefice, P., 81–82, 87
O'Reilly, M. R., 23, 26

Orellana, I., 79, 85, 88
Orr, D. W., 23, 26, 44, 45, 70, 71, 72, 78
O'Sullivan, E., 17–18, 21, 23, 24, 26, 82, 88, 95

Parajuli, P., 49, 50, 57
Parks, S. D., 23, 25
Participatory research, 33
Patrick, K., 2, 59, 68, 90, 91–92
Peasant movements, 50, 85–86
Pedagogies of environment, 81–82
Pedagogy of place, 81
Pipe, P., 73, 77
Plaskow, J., 22, 26
Plumwood, V., 19, 21, 26
Podu, 52–53
Polaris Institute, 11
Popular education: defined, 47; democratic participation and, 47–48. See also Environmental popular education
Porter, M., 84, 87
Poverty: globalization and, 7, 9–10, 40; in postindependence India, 48–49, 51
Pow Wow Highway, 63
Power, relations between knowledge and, 47, 52–55
Praxis based approach, 85
"Principles of Collaboration," 28
Privatization, 41
Production, capitalist, 7–8
Protectionism, 40–41
Protests. See Activism; Resistance; Social movements and protests
Public education interventions, 83–84
Public policy: community sustainability and, 40, 42–45; grassroots movement learning and, 30–31, 34–36
Pula, 20

Racism, 1, 2; environmental, 9–10, 28, 31–32, 35; globalization and, 9–10
Raging Grannies, 34
Rao, M.S.A., 49, 57
Ratinoff, L., 20, 26
Readings, on environmental adult education, 93–95
Redclift, M., 40, 45
Redwood Retirement Center, California, 12
Reflexive modernization, 82
Reflexivity, 66, 67, 82
Religion, 1
Research, participatory, 33

Resistance: environmental adult education about, 12; by indigenous people movements, 50. *See also* Activism; Social movements and protests
Resnick, L. B., 84, 87
Rifkin, J., 8, 15
Rio+5, 79
Risk society, 82
Ritual, 52–53, 63, 64–65, 67
Rizvi, S., 48, 57
Robichon, P., 85, 88
Robottom, I., 83, 88
Robyn, L., 35, 37
Roth, C. E., 69–70, 77, 78
Rothwell, W. J., 80, 88
Routledge, P., 49, 50, 57
Rowe, S., 8, 15
Roy, C., 34, 37
Roy, S., 48, 57

Sachs, C. E., 40, 45, 55
Sachs, W., 57
St. Clair, R., 3, 69, 78, 90–91, 92, 93
Salazar, D., 34, 37
Salmon, J., 75, 77
Sandilands, C., 10, 15
Sandweiss, S., 31, 37
Saro-Wiwa, K., 7
Sauvé, L., 83, 85, 88
Schön, D., 79, 88
Schrecker, T., 19, 26
Schugurensky, D., 47, 54, 57
Science, 3; critique of, 32–33, 53–54, 73–75, 90–91; cultural politics of, 32–33, 53–54; language and metaphor of, 22
Scientific education, environmental literacy and, 3, 71–73
Senge, P. M., 80, 88
Serrano, I., 43, 44, 45
Sexism, 1, 2; environmental, 9–10; feminist ecology and, 18–19; globalization and, 9–10
Sexton, K., 27, 37
Sexual orientation, 1, 28
Shah, G., 49, 57
Shaker, E., 41, 45
Shell, 7
Shiva, V., 9, 15, 19, 21, 26, 50, 56
Sierra Leone civil war, 7
Simpson, L., 10, 12, 15
Singh, K. S., 49, 50, 57
Sklair, L., 55, 57

Smith, B., 40, 45
Smyth, J., 89, 95
Social change, 1; environmental justice (EJ) movement and, 27–36, 76–77; grassroots movement learning and, 30–31, 34–36, 75–77; integrating environmental issues into, 17–18, 24–25, 27–36; spirituality and, 23. *See also* Activism; Resistance; Social movements and protests
Social ecology, 19
Social injustices, 1, 2; environmental justice and, 28–29, 34–36; globalization and, 6–7, 91–92. *See also* Oppression
Social instability: development and, 48–49; globalization and, 5, 6–7, 9–10
Social movement learning, 2, 11, 30–31, 34–36, 75–77, 92–93; in indigenous social movements, 47–55, 76–77, 92. *See also* Environmental popular education
Social movements and protests: antiglobalization, 7, 12–13, 33–34, 85–86, 92–93; environmental adult education and, 12–13, 75–77, 92–93; environmental justice and, 27–28, 30–31, 34–36, 76–77; environmental popular education and, 47–55, 75–77; women's, 11–12, 63–64, 66, 86. *See also* Activism
Social science, 72
Socioeconomic class, 1, 2
Soil fertility, 54
Soreng, N., 51, 57
Species arrogance, 20
Spirituality, 2, 22–23, 92; ritual and, 64–65
Spretnak, C., 72, 74, 77
Sproull, L. S., 80, 87
Stalker, J., 11, 15
Stannett, A., 82, 87
State responsibility, 13
Sterling, S., 82, 88
Stromquist, N., 6, 15, 33, 37
Sullivan, E., 47, 56
"Summary of Accomplishments of the Environmental Justice Networks," 27, 37
Sumner, J., 2, 19, 39, 40, 45, 90, 91, 93
Supporting Women for Economics, the Environment, and Popular Education (SWEEPE), 60–67; background of, 60–61; observations of, 61–62; pat-

terns of, 62–65; working conclusions of, 65–67; workings of, 61
Sustainability, defined, 42–43. *See also* Community sustainability; Environmental sustainability
SWEEPE. *See* Supporting Women for Economics, the Environment, and Popular Education (SWEEPE)

Tan, S., 12, 15, 93–94
Targeted public education, 83–84
Teach-ins, 11, 33
Theater, 11, 12
Thomashow, M., 18, 19, 21, 26
Thompson, J. L., 67, 68
Thukral, E., 49, 56
Tiger economies, 40
Tisdell, E. J., 23, 26
Tompkins, J., 24, 26
Toronto Chinese Health Education Committee, 12
Toxic Wastes in the United States, 38
Toxics Watch, 27, 38
Transformative Learning (O'Sullivan), 95
Transmission, 90–91
Tripathi, R., 48, 57
Tucker, R. C., 6, 15
Tuijnman, A. 80, 87

Uganda, ecological literacy program in, 12
UNESCO, 70, 77, 83, 88
UNICEF, 83, 88
United Church of Christ Commission for Racial Justice, 27, 38
United Nations (UN), 13, 79, 83, 92
United Nations (UN) Conference on Environment and Development, 27, 79, 83
United Nations (UN) Development Programme, 49, 57
United Nations (UN) Environmental Programs (UNEP), 83
United States: consumerism in, 59–60; environmental adult education in, 1; environmental justice (EJ) movements in, 27, 76–77; grassroots education in, 30; participatory action research in, 33
Universities: environmental adult education in, 11, 31; social justice education in, 36
University of Calgary, 11
University of Waikato, New Zealand, 11

Urban renewal, 82
U.S. Environmental Protection Agency (EPA), 28
U.S. Subcommittee on Civil and Constitutional Rights, 28

Vaill, P., 24, 26
Vancouver Island, Canada, 11–12
Vandenabeele, J., 75, 77
Vella, J., 23, 26
Viezzer, M., 12, 15, 30, 38
Vocationalization, 41
Von Moltke, K., 8, 15

Wagner, S., 80, 88
Wall, R., 31, 38
War: globalization and, 5, 6–7, 12; movement and protests against, 12, 31
Washington University, Center for the Study of American Business, 32
Watkins, K. E., 80, 88
Waye, N., 86
Welton, M., 18, 26, 30, 38
Wenger, E., 79, 82, 85, 87, 88
Westwood, S., 81, 87
Whalen, J., 82, 88
Whelan, J., 13, 15
Whitaker, T., 12, 15
Wilber, K., 20–21, 23, 26
Wildemeersch, D., 75, 77
William, R., 81
Women, 2; consumerism and, 59–60; ecological literacy program for, 12; environmental justice and, 35; environmental popular education for, 59–67; feminist philosophies and, 12, 19, 21; globalization and, 9–10, 91; movements and protests of, 11–12, 63–64, 66; SWEEP Project of, 60–67
Work environments, 80
World Bank (WB), 33, 40, 83
World Commission on Environment and Development, 79, 88
World Summit on Sustainable Development, 27–28
World Trade Organization (WTO), 33
Worldviews, 20; environmental learning and, 43–44; environmental literacy and, 72; fractured, 20–21, 22, 92; indigenous, 52–53

Ziaka, Y., 85, 88
Zimmerman, M. E., 19, 26

Back Issue/Subscription Order Form

Copy or detach and send to:
Jossey-Bass, A Wiley Company, 989 Market Street, San Francisco CA 94103-1741

Call or fax toll-free: Phone 888-378-2537 6:30AM – 3PM PST; Fax 888-481-2665

Back Issues: Please send me the following issues at $27 each
(Important: please include ISBN number with your order.)

_____

_____

_____

$ _____   Total for single issues

$ _____   SHIPPING CHARGES: SURFACE   Domestic Canadian

	First Item	$5.00	$6.00
	Each Add'l Item	$3.00	$1.50

For next-day and second-day delivery rates, call the number listed above.

Subscriptions: Please _start _renew my subscription to *New Directions for Adult and Continuing Education* for the year 2_____at the following rate:

U.S.	_ Individual $70	_ Institutional $149
Canada	_ Individual $70	_ Institutional $189
All Others	_ Individual $94	_ Institutional $223
Online Subscription		_ Institutional $149

**For more information about online subscriptions visit
www.interscience.wiley.com**

$ _____   Total single issues and subscriptions (Add appropriate sales tax for your state for single issue orders. No sales tax for U.S. subscriptions. Canadian residents, add GST for subscriptions and single issues.)

_ Payment enclosed (U.S. check or money order only)
_ VISA _MC _AmEx _# _____ Exp. Date _____

Signature _____ Day Phone _____
_ Bill Me (U.S. institutional orders only. Purchase order required.)

Purchase order # _____
    Federal Tax ID13559302   GST 89102 8052

Name _____

Address _____

_____

Phone _____ E-mail _____

For more information about Jossey-Bass, visit our Web site at www.josseybass.com

PROMOTION CODE ND03

OTHER TITLES AVAILABLE IN THE
NEW DIRECTIONS FOR ADULT AND CONTINUING EDUCATION SERIES
Susan Imel, Jovita M. Ross-Gordon, COEDITORS-IN-CHIEF

ACE98   New Perspectives on Designing and Implementing Professional
Development of Teachers of Adults
Kathleen P. King, Patricia A. Lawler
ISBN 0-7879-6918-4

ACE97   Accelerated Learning for Adults: The Promise and Practice of Intensive
Educational Formats
Raymond J. Wlodkowski, Carol E. Kasworm
ISBN 0-7879-6794-7

ACE96   Learning and Sociocultural Contexts: Implications for Adults,
Community, and Workplace Education
Mary V. Alfred
ISBN 0-7879-6326-7

ACE95   Adult Learning in Community
Susan Imel, David Stein
ISBN 0-7879-6323-2

ACE94   Collaborative Inquiry as a Strategy for Adult Learning
Lyle Yorks, Elizabeth Kasl
ISBN 0-7879-6322-4

ACE93   Contemporary Viewpoints on Teaching Adults Effectively
Jovita Ross-Gordon
ISBN 0-7879-6229-5

ACE92   Sociocultural Perspectives on Learning through Work
Tara Fenwick
ISBN 0-7879-5775-5

ACE91   Understanding and Negotiating the Political Landscape of Adult Education
Catherine A. Hansman, Peggy A. Sissel
ISBN 0-7879-5775-5

ACE90   Promoting Journal Writing in Adult Education
Leona M. English, Marie A. Gillen
ISBN 0-7879-5774-7

ACE89   The New Update on Adult Learning Theory
Sharan B. Merriam
ISBN 0-7879-5773-9

ACE88   Strategic Use of Learning Technologies
Elizabeth J. Burge
ISBN 0-7879-5426-8

ACE87   Team Teaching and Learning in Adult Education
Mary-Jane Eisen, Elizabeth J. Tisdell
ISBN 0-7879-5425-X

ACE86   Charting a Course for Continuing Professional Education: Reframing
        Professional Practice
        Vivian W. Mott, Barbara J. Daley
        ISBN 0-7879-5424-1

ACE85   Addressing the Spiritual Dimensions of Adult Learning: What Educators
        Can Do
        Leona M. English, Marie A. Gillen
        ISBN 0-7879-5364-4

ACE84   An Update on Adult Development Theory: New Ways of Thinking About
        the Life Course
        M. Carolyn Clark, Rosemary J. Caffarella
        ISBN 0-7879-1171-2

ACE83   The Welfare-to-Work Challenge for Adult Literacy Educators
        Larry G. Martin, James C. Fisher
        ISBN 0-7879-1170-4

ACE82   Providing Culturally Relevant Adult Education: A Challenge for the
        Twenty-First Century
        Talmadge C. Guy
        ISBN 0-7879-1167-4

ACE79   The Power and Potential of Collaborative Learning Partnerships
        Iris M. Saltiel, Angela Sgroi, Ralph G. Brockett
        ISBN 0-7879-9815-X

ACE77   Using Learning to Meet the Challenges of Older Adulthood
        James C. Fisher, Mary Alice Wolf
        ISBN 0-7879-1164-X

ACE75   Assessing Adult Learning in Diverse Settings: Current Issues and
        Approaches
        ISBN 0-7879-9840-0

ACE70   A Community-Based Approach to Literacy Programs: Taking Learners'
        Lives into Account
        Peggy A. Sissel
        ISBN 0-7879-9867-2

ACE66   Mentoring: New Strategies and Challenges
        Michael W. Galbraith, Norman H. Cohen
        ISBN 0-7879-9912-1

ACE59   Applying Cognitive Learning Theory to Adult Learning
        Daniele D. Flannery
        ISBN 1-55542-716-2

ACE57   An Update on Adult Learning Theory
        Sharan B. Merriam
        ISBN 1-55542-684-0

**NEW DIRECTIONS FOR
ADULT AND CONTINUING EDUCATION
IS NOW AVAILABLE ONLINE AT WILEY INTERSCIENCE**

What is Wiley InterScience?

Wiley InterScience is the dynamic online content service from John Wiley & Sons delivering the full text of over 300 leading scientific, technical, medical, and professional journals, plus major reference works, the acclaimed *Current Protocols* laboratory manuals, and even the full text of select Wiley print books online.

What are some special features of Wiley InterScience?

Wiley InterScience Alerts is a service that delivers table of contents via e-mail for any journal available on Wiley InterScience as soon as a new issue is published online.
Early View is Wiley's exclusive service presenting individual articles online as soon as they are ready, even before the release of the compiled print issue. These articles are complete, peer-reviewed, and citable.
CrossRef is the innovative multi-publisher reference linking system enabling readers to move seamlessly from a reference in a journal article to the cited publication, typically located on a different server and published by a different publisher.

How can I access Wiley InterScience?

Visit http://www.interscience.wiley.com

Guest Users can browse Wiley InterScience for unrestricted access to journal Tables of Contents and Article Abstracts, or use the powerful search engine.
Registered Users are provided with a *Personal Home Page* to store and manage customized alerts, searches, and links to favorite journals and articles. Additionally, Registered Users can view free Online Sample Issues and preview selected material from major reference works.
Licensed Customers are entitled to access full-text journal articles in PDF, with select journals also offering full-text HTML.

How do I become an Authorized User?

Authorized Users are individuals authorized by a paying Customer to have access to the journals in Wiley InterScience. For example, a university that subscribes to Wiley journals is considered to be the Customer. Faculty, staff and students authorized by the university to have access to those journals in Wiley InterScience are Authorized Users. Users should contact their Library for information on which Wiley journals they have access to in Wiley InterScience.

ASK YOUR INSTITUTION ABOUT WILEY INTERSCIENCE TODAY!